SECRETS
OF WINNING
SLOTS

THE POWERFUL & EASY-TO-LEARN GUIDE TO BEATING SLOTS AND WALIKING AWAY WITH THE CASINO'S MONEY!

AVERY CARDOZA

SECRETS OF WINNING SLOTS

OF WINNING SLOTS

THE POWERFUL & EASY-TO-LEARN GUIDE TO BEATING SLOTS
AND WALIKING AWAY WITH THE CASINO'S MONEY!

AVERY CARDOZA

CARDOZA PUBLISHING

Cardoza Publishing is the foremost gaming and gambling publisher in the world with a library of almost 200 up-to-date and easy-to-read books and strategies. These authoritative works are written by the top experts in their fields and with more than 10 million books in print, represent the best-selling and most popular gaming books anywhere.

NEW EDITION

Copyright © 1998, 2003, 2016 by Avery Cardoza
All Rights Reserved

Library of Congress Catalog Number: 2016940239
ISBN 10: 1-58042-338-8   ISBN 13: 978-1-58042-338-0

Visit our new web site (www.cardozabooks.com) or write us
for a full list of books, advanced and computer strategies.

CARDOZA PUBLISHING
P.O. Box 98115, Las Vegas, NV 89193
Toll Free Phone (800)577-WINS
email: cardozabooks@aol.com
www.cardozabooks.com

ABOUT THE AUTHOR

Avery Cardoza, the world's foremost authority on gambling and a million-selling author of more than 50 books and advanced strategies, is the founder of Cardoza Publishing (publisher of more than 200 gaming titles, 10 million copies sold) and owner of the legendary Gambler's Book Club and iconic Gambler's General Store in Las Vegas. Millions of gamblers have learned how to play and win money at gambling following his no-nonsense practical advice.

Cardoza has been studying numbers and winning systems since he was five-years old. He has developed the most powerful lottery software and strategies ever formulated including the only systems using powerful Level II keys such as kings, wizards, and courts, and Level III advanced strategies found nowhere else. Cardoza is one of the foremost experts on predictive randomness for lotteries, the heart and soul of strategies that have won players millions upon millions of dollars. His work on lotto and lottery strategies includes the powerful *Lottery Super System*, the "bible" on beating lotto and lottery, *Secrets of Winning Lotto & Lottery*, and more than a dozen specialized Level III advanced strategies.

Cardoza's work is the centerpiece of LotterySuperSystem.com, the powerful online site for casual and serious players looking to win millions of dollars at lotto and lottery games.

TABLE OF CONTENTS

STRATEGY CHARTS & CALL-OUTS

INTRODUCTION

I'm going to show you how to get the most fun from playing your favorite slot machines and in the process, give yourself the best chances of winning jackpots!

That's right, the goal of this book is for you to win jackpots!

Can you win at slots? Of course, but only if you know how to put the odds on your side. Many players have misconceptions about playing slot machines. I'm not only going to dispel these and focus on how to work the machines in your favor, but also how to take advantage of the free rooms, free meals, free tickets to the best shows in town, and the other goodies casinos offer to their good slots players including cash back on your play!

I'll show you how to find the best machines, how to guarantee that winning sessions remain winners, how to minimize losing sessions, how to find the machines that pay the highest returns, and how to avoid ones that attract suckers like sitting ducks. Once you know how to get all the freebies that the casinos have to offer, and learned the secrets I'm going to reveal to you in this book, you may have earned yourself a free vacation doing exactly what you like to do—playing and beating the casino at slots.

Read on—it's time to learn the secrets of winning slots!

THE GROUND GAME

There is nothing like bells, whistles, eruptions and catchy music emanating from a hot slot machine or a bunch of hot slot machines to generate excitement and electricity to all slots players within earshot of the racket, and to get these people thinking that they too want to catch a winner.

The sounds of winning are contagious. It's like laughter. The more players that hear the sounds of winning, the greater the draw it is for players and non-players alike to want in on the action. They're thinking, "The machines are hot and paying," and the noise draws them toward the source. Soon, a portion of these bystanders become players, ready to park themselves in front of nearby machines, ready take their chances.

Welcome to Las Vegas, the Indian casinos, Atlantic City, riverboats, and the endless other venues where the slots are king. No longer are the slot machines just a noisy profit center for the casinos. They now generate more than 50% of the average casino's income, and in casinos that only have slot machines on their floors (known as **slots palaces**), they make up a full 100% of the gambling income.

The temptation of playing for monster jackpots combined with the allure of gambling has turned the slot machine business into a multi-billion dollar industry. Walking through a casino and seeing the mania surrounding endless banks of machines is simply awe-inspiring for first time visitors. The noise, flashing lights, and video displays of winning machines is hard to resist.

Interestingly, one major difference between slots players and other casino-goers is that slots players generally play their machines without too many illusions. They play for fun with no serious expectations of winning. The game is relaxing for them, especially fun when winning, but the bottom line is that they know the casino has the edge and will probably take some of their money. Just the same, they can have a good time.

Many other gamblers—the players who take on the table games—know that the casinos have an edge, but still believe that they're somehow going to beat the odds. Some of these gamblers are even convinced that they're going to win. Paycheck after paycheck goes into these beliefs, the casinos build more spectacular facades and larger towers, and more mega-resorts get constructed every year with upwards of 4,000 rooms to feast on gamblers. And yet, the dream of the dreamers still doesn't fade.

Slots players are more realistic in their approach. Their dream of hitting the big one is tempered by the fact that they know the casino is going to win, ultimately. But if they get lucky, and the reels line up in their favor, oh, that could be sweet.

The goal of this book is to educate you, not only about the slot machines in all their aspects, but also about the realities of gambling. Misconceptions abound and I want to remove them from your mind so that you approach the machines with cold hard facts on your side, all illusions scattered to the winds.

Let's start with the basics. Gambling is about risking money, and in a casino, with few exceptions, the odds are against you. This means that you should expect to lose money when you play. You also have the possibility of winning, and the slim possibility of winning very, very big. But the fact remains: If you gamble long enough, you'll probably lose. The law of odds says so; every luxury casino built on losers' money says so; empirical evidence says so. And what's more, deep down, when sanity rears its wizened eyes, every gambler knows it.

THE LONG RUN AND THE SHORT RUN

The slot machines you play in the casinos have been set so that, mathematically, they will show a profit to the casino in the long run. I will show you techniques and strategies to bring those odds down to the bare minimum, and money management strategies that will allow you to beat the machines in the short run. But the raw fact is that your expectation is to lose money in the long run. There is no way around it. Not every slots player will lose, for luck shows winners sometimes, but just about everyone who plays for any length of time will be ground down by the odds and will lose money.

You need to play with a full understanding of what you can and can't do. The goal is to bring the odds down to the bare minimum, and when you're winning, to take the money as profits. The higher goal is to put yourself in the position to also have fun, and that means to bet within your means so that no possible run of bad luck can really hurt you, financially or emotionally. I will talk a lot about money management in this book because there is nothing more important to the slots player.

Fortunately for you, there are ways to cash in on the casino's eagerness to draw you in, and this leads to good things, such as free meals, shows, rooms, giveaways, cash rebates and more. I'll show you how to take advantage of playing the slots.

Let's learn a little more about the machines first.

THE SLOT MACHINE

Slot machines are composed of various functioning parts. It will help to be familiar with them. I'll go over them here.

THE MACHINE

The Reels

The spinning mechanism on slot machines that contain symbols are the reels, technically known as stepper reels for the various "steps" or "stops." Classic slot machines, like IGT's Red/White/Blue have three reels, as the earliest machines did back when Fey invented them. Modern slot machines have five reels—all penny slots do—and are generally referred to as "video" slots. Specialty machines, mostly novelty-type slots, have as many as ten reels and are often referred to as Big Berthas.

Each reel on the older generations of slot machine contain a number of steps or stops, places where the wheel can end when it is spun. This stop may contain a symbol such as a cherry or lemon on classic three-reel machines, or it may even contain a blank, a stop with no symbol.

The stops on video five-reel machines contain symbols such as animals or people and contain no blanks.

Before slots with microcomputer chips were introduced, the typical reels contained twenty to twenty-four stops. Multiplying the classic three-reel machine by twenty stops per reel gave the machines a total of 8,000 combinations: 20 x 20 x 20. Machines that used twenty-four reels offered a possibility for slots operators to determine their winning payouts according to a total number of 13,824 chances.

Of course, whether there are a total of 8,000 combinations or 13,824 combinations makes no difference to a player's winning chances. It is all determined by the likelihood of hitting winning combinations, and the amount that is awarded when they occur. The slot manufacturer establishes both of these factors according to the purchaser's specifications.

Nowadays, with winning combinations determined by sophisticated programs that emulate random spins, reels contain as many as 128 stops, which gives manufacturers much greater flexibility in setting and adjusting the payout schedules and frequency of hits they'll offer to the players. The classic 128-stop machine contains twenty-two actual symbols and 106 blanks.

On this new generation of microchip video machines, the concept of a stop differs from the electromechanical and earlier predecessors in that the "stop" is no longer necessarily a physical place where the reel stops, but a simulated place. There was no need to create 106 blank stops using a computer chip. Rather, the program would simulate a wheel containing 106 blanks to go along with the twenty-two symbols. The frequency of hits and number of payouts would be set by the program designer, and that total combination of possibilities, as set by the manufacturer, would determine the percentage payout that might be expected by the player.

To loosen or tighten the machine, all the casino has to do is or reset the programming or replace the computer chip with a new one, and the deed is done.

The Payline

The glass panel mounted on the front of a classic slot machine's reels is marked by a horizontal line, called a payline. Winning combinations must line up directly behind this line for the spin to be a paying winner. If winning symbols line up, but they're not directly behind the payline, the spin is not a winner.

Some classic machines have three or five paylines. When there are three paylines, they will generally be lined up as three horizontals, one in the middle and one each above and below that line. Usually, it takes one coin for each payline to be activated. Machines with five paylines usually add two diagonal paylines. These slots need the full five coins for all paylines to be active.

Modern video slot machines typically have twenty to forty paylines, with some machines having up to one hundred paylines. You select the number of paylines you want to be activated and the number of coins to be played on each payline.

The Payout Display

On the top of each classic slot machine is a payout display with a colorful attractive design listing the winning combinations that can be spun and the number of coins or dollar amount that will be paid when there is a winner. Other special winning combinations or conditions are printed there as well.

The payout display on classic machines shows the winning payouts for every coin played, and if the machine is a progressive, it either shows the progressive total on the machine itself, or is marked "Progressive." When "Progressive" is indicated on the payout display, that jackpot total will be prominently displayed on a large display sign above the bank of progressive machines.

On video slot machines with multiple paylines, the player must push a button commonly labeled PAYOUTS to view all the winning combinations.

Service Light

On top of each slot machine is a red indicator light, known as the Service Light, which will light up whenever the service of a slots employee is needed. The red light will be activated when the player presses the CHANGE button requesting assistance, when the machine malfunctions, or when a jackpot is hit and the machine is unable to payout the full amount of the win. The last condition is the one I really like to see, that and all the noise that comes with it.

The Slots Handle

The slots handle is a vestige of the past. Only a few slot machines, primarily classic progressives, still have a long handle, though far smaller than vintage handles, located on their right side that you can pull to spin the reels, provided that you have enough credits to play, of course. No credits, no play. Pulling the handle used to be the only way you could activate the reels to spin and is still preferred by some players, even with the advent of the easier, faster credit buttons on modern machines.

While the result of pulling the slots handle is exactly the same as when it was first created almost 100 years ago, there is a major difference in its actual functionality. Originally, pulling the handle would mechanically set the reels in motion. Nowadays it does no such thing. Slot machines are microchip units and are not mechanically triggered. Pulling the handle on modern machines activates the software, which sets the reels in motion—a quantum difference from the pre-80s machines.

The metal coin tray is also a vestige of the past. Mounted on the bottom of machines, the tray used to catch the coins that would pour out of classic slot machines when you pushed the CASH OUT button. Today's modern machines spit out vouchers that you can exchange for cash at designated machines, at the cashier's cage, or play in another machine. We'll talk more about how payout vouchers (TICKETS) work later.

THE PLAY BUTTONS

In this section, I describe the active play buttons you might find on a slot machine. Note that depending on the manufacturer, some of the buttons listed may have slightly different names, but in general, they serve the same function.

Spin Reels

When money is inserted into the machine, or less than the full amount of credits are played, you will have to manually press the SPIN REELS button to get the action going.

Play Max Credits

Pressing the PLAY MAX CREDITS button will play the full amount of credits allowed by the machine and automatically spin the reels. Thus, if the machine accepts five coins as a bet, pressing PLAY MAX CREDITS will deduct five coins from your credits. Similarly, if three coins were the maximum bet, then three coins would be played and that amount would be deducted. The PLAY MAX CREDITS button will only activate the reels (and deduct the coins played) if enough credits are in the machine. If there aren't enough credits in the machine, you will have to insert more money into the heart of the beast and play off of those credits.

If you do not have enough credits left to make your desired bet on a video slot machine, a message may flash across the screen, reading "Insert More Credits or Change Selection."

Play Two Credits, Play Three Credits

On some classic machines that accept two credits or three credits, you may see a button that states PLAY TWO CREDITS or PLAY THREE CREDITS. These buttons serve the same function as the PLAY MAX CREDITS button. For example, if you see PLAY TWO CREDITS on a machine, that machine most likely accepts two coins as the maximum bet. Pressing the button would deduct two from your credits and spin the reels.

Play One Credit

For players who prefer playing one credit at a time, classic slots generally have a PLAY ONE CREDIT button. Pressing this button will play one credit toward the next pull, but will not automatically activate the reels, as the PLAY MAX CREDITS button does. Nothing will happen. The reels will not spin until the SPIN REELS button is pressed.

You can also play two credits by pressing the PLAY ONE CREDIT button twice, or play three credits by pressing it three times, and so on until the full allowance of credits the machine allows is reached.

Repeat the Bet

If you intend to play the same amount of credits on your next spin as you did on your previous spin, you can press the REPEAT THE BET button. Pressing this button relieves you of having to enter the amount of your bet each time and speeds up your play.

Take Win Button (Cash Out Button)

When pressed on vintage classic machines, the CASH OUT button converted all the credits accrued during the playing session into coins that dropped like a metal waterfall into the coin tray below. For players that prefer things the way they were in the old days, some Las Vegas casinos provide a small area filled with vintage machines that spit out coins when the Cash Out button is pressed.

The industry standard these days is that accrued credits are issued in the form of a payout voucher commonly called a TICKET. All modern video slot machines convert accrued credits into a ticket that can be redeemed for money, or inserted into another machine. These machines, and this process, are called Ticket-In/Ticket-Out (TITO).

As soon as the machine issues the payout voucher, it prompts you to immediately remove the ticket by displaying the message "Collect Ticket." Players may exchange tickets for cash at one of the designated conversion machines on the casino floor, or at the casino cashier's cage.

Players use the TAKE WIN (CASH OUT) button when they're ready to change machines, call it a day at the slots, or simply hear the whirr of a winning ticket being spit out of the machine. In the old days when classic machines ruled the roost, you'd hear the victory charge of coins pounding into the coin tray. No matter how you receive your payout, the sound of money won is always fun to hear!

ADVANTAGES AND DISADVANTAGES OF TICKET-IN/TICKET-OUT SLOT MACHINES

ADVANTAGES
1. TITO machines are a lot cleaner than coin machines. Money is dirty, especially coins, so you don't have to continually wash your hands or worry about getting your clothes dirty. You may also find the casino floor to be cleaner—no plastic buckets or coin racks to clut-

ter spaces between machines, no paper wrappers from rolls of coins littering the floor.

2. TITO machines are much faster and more convenient than coin machines. No waiting at a machine for an attendant to refill it with coins when the beast doesn't have enough in its belly to drop the full amount of your payout. No waiting at the cashier's cage to convert your coins into bills. No waiting for the hopper to swirl round and round tallying your coins, or waiting for the cashier to refill the hopper.

3. You don't have to haul heavy buckets of quarters or racks of dollar tokens around with them.

4. TITO machines automatically pay out up to $1,199 on a single spin, and more than that on cumulative spins of less than $1,199 each. So, unless you hit a jackpot of $1,200 or more, there's no need to wait for an attendant, although, in that case, you really don't mind the wait.

DISADVANTAGES
1. Tickets can fool you into not remembering that they are the same as cash, so you can play more money than you intended to play.

2. When a TITO machine runs out of paper or malfunctions and thus cannot issue a payout voucher, you will have to wait for a slots attendant to solve the problem. Casinos don't need to employ nearly as many slots attendants as they did in the old days, so there may be quite a wait for help.

3. Tickets can easily be misplaced.

The Change Button or Service Button

On the far left position on the button display will be a CHANGE or SERVICE button that brings you door-to-door service from a slots attendant, often called a changeperson. Pressing this button lights up the red service light on the top of your machine and lets the slots attendants know that you need service.

I remember when I learned first hand about the function of the change button. Way back in my early days studying the strategies for beating the slots I was interviewing the slots manager at a small, off-strip casino while seated at one of the slots. I was on a stool, leaning with my back against the machine, facing the slots manager who stood behind me.

He was busy explaining his knowledge of the slots, which, just as typical of casino employees as with players, was rife with misconceptions.

In the middle of the conversation, a changeperson came by, interrupted the manager's conversation with a half joking remark, reached over me to hit a button on the machine, and moved on again. Thinking she was play-acting a spin of the reels, I thought nothing of it. Our conversation continued with the same scenario repeating itself a few minutes later, and then a third time after that. I couldn't figure out why the changeperson kept interrupting the manager.

It was only later, while I was studying the machine's design, I think it was an IGT Red, White and Blue, that I realized I had been leaning on the change button, and a changeperson had hurriedly come over each time, only to find that her services weren't needed.

So that's what was going on! Those change buttons do work.

THE DISPLAYS

There will be several displays on the front of the machine. While different slots may display the information in different locations, the basic information will be part of any modern slot machine.

Credits Played

The Credits Played display shows how many credits are being bet on a particular spin. Thus, if twenty credits are played, the display would indicate the number "20."

Credits

The Credits indicator shows how many credits you have accumulated, either through winning spins or through money entered into the machine. Each credit shown will reflect the denomination of coin you're playing. For example, placing a $20 bill into a 25¢ classic machine will enter eighty 25¢ credits into your account. The Credits indicator will read "80." If you play three credits from that total, the Credits will read "77." If that spin is a win for twenty credits, the Credits will now read "97" to reflect the twenty coins won. If you put $20 into a penny machine, the credits will indicate "2000."

Pushing the PLAY ONE CREDIT button automatically deducts one credit from your remaining credits, while PLAY MAX CREDITS deducts the maximum amount of credits you are allowed to wager on any one spin.

You can use your credits by either playing them until the total is down to 0 (which means you've lost them all), parlaying them into a giant win, or by hitting the TAKE WIN button, which will convert your credits into a payout voucher for the actual dollar amount you have won.

Winner Paid

The Winner Paid indicator displays the amount won on the current spin. For example, if 200 credits are won, the machine will read "200."

Error Code

Yet another indicator on the front of the machine is the Error Code indicator. Should the machine malfunction in some fashion, the error code indicator will display a code number that alerts a slots technician to the nature of the problem so that he can address it and fix your machine.

THE SYMBOLS

Remarkably, many of the slot machine symbols have survived since they were first popularized back in the early part of the twentieth century. The Liberty Bell symbol, found on the original Fey slots machine of 1899, can still be found on machines today!

What stands out among successful slot machines is the simplicity of the symbols. Cherries, lemons, sevens, liberty bells—all basic symbols familiar to slots players—have struck a chord over time. These basic symbols have long histories dating back more than fifty years and somehow continue to hold strong even today.

Another prevalent symbol in the classic machines is the bar. Machines often feature bars in various forms and colors: single bars, double bars, and triple bars. A popular payout on classic slot machines is the Any Bar symbol. This means that any bar shown can be used in combination with any of the other bars to create a winner.

There are many more symbols as well nowadays, especially with the large proliferation of slot machine manufacturers and machines that are made for current trends. In addition to the basic symbols discussed above, there are symbols galore to be found, from other fruits, numbers, and styles of bars, to a wide variety of "theme" machines with endless symbols created by designers ever eager to hit a machine that catches hold of enough players to be successful.

In addition to the printed symbols on classic slots machine are other stops, or blanks, which are simply blank spaces on the reel and have no winning potential. Modern five-reel video slot machines do not have blanks.

Wild Symbols

Wild symbols are used in the designs of many machines. Certain machines will designate a particular symbol as "wild," which means that the wild symbol can be used as any symbol on the machine to create a winning combination. For example, BAR BAR Wild, would give you a payout for three bars on a classic slot.

On a five-reel video slot, the wild symbol may be anything from a butterfly to a pot of gold.

Some machines use the wild symbols to multiply the player's payout line. For example, on IGT's classic Double Diamond machine, the diamond symbol, when lined up to form a winning combination, will double the payout. Two diamonds are even better, as they will double each other for four times the payout.

Bonus and Free Game Symbols

Popular features of many penny slot machines are the bonus and free game symbols. When enough of these symbols line up, you get free spins on the wheels, and sometimes winning multipliers as well. When you start hitting the free spins on the penny machines, the extra rounds can add up to a good number of credits.

THE BASICS OF PLAY

Playing a slot machine is quite easy. It is no more compli-cated than putting a ticket or money in the machine and either pressing the "SPIN REELS" button or pulling the handle on the old classic machines. As the machines have become more sophisticated throughout the years, additional features have been added to make playing slots even easier.

This chapter will cover all the basics of play and general infor-mation you need to know to get set up at the machines, and to use the various features available. Let's start by understanding what you're trying to do.

OBJECT OF THE GAME

The goal in slots is to get the symbols on the reels to line up directly behind the payline in one of the winning combina-tions listed on the front of the machine. The higher ranked the combination, as listed, the greater the payout will be.

The real goal in slots is to hit the jackpot paying thousands of dollars, tens of thousands of dollars, or even millions of dol-lars on the big progressives, that is, to hit the jackpot! Then it's off to Hawaii for a year or more as the first stop on your post-retirement trans-world luxury cruise; the ability to do whatever you want, whenever you want, without answering to anyone anymore. Not a bad goal.

PLAYING THE SLOTS
Bills and Coins
The easiest way to play slots is by inserting bills or tickets that have cash credits directly into the machine and playing the

credits according to the amount of money value you have inserted. The device that accepts your money is called a bill acceptor. Slots normally accept $1, $5, $20, $50 and $100 bills, which are converted directly into credits on the machine and allow you to play carefree for as long as you still have credits available.

In the not too distant past, going directly to a change booth set up in or near the slots area, or tracking down one of the many changepeople who patrolled the machines wheeling carts full of change, was how you used to get coins so you could play the machines. You also could press the CHANGE button located on the left side of the machine, which would light up the red bulb atop the machine and alert changepeople to come with coins. However, playing by actual coins is a relic of the past.

While there are a few machines that can still be played with coins, the models being manufactured nowadays take only paper money or paper tickets that you have cashed out from a ticket-in/ticket-out machine. Ticket-in/ticket-out machines pay you with bar-coded paper tickets that denote the amount of money you have earned at cash-out time. These tickets can be inserted into another machine for their cash value, or can be converted into actual cash at the casino cashier cage. You'll find them in all modern casinos.

Coin Denominations

Slot machines can be played in a variety of denominations. You can play the small coin machines, 1¢, 5¢, 10¢, and 25¢; the medium coin machines, 50¢ or $1; or the big coin machines, $5, $25, $100, and even $500 slots! You read that right. There are $500 slot machines out there and they do get action from some very high rolling players looking for a major score!

The 25¢ and $1 machines are popular among players, but without doubt, the king (or queen) or all machines today is the penny slots. The introduction of 1¢ machines has proved to be genius. These penny slots are wildly popular and dominate the slots areas. But since players can play multiple credits, even as many as 100 per spin or more, these penny machines are really $1 machines and higher in disguise.

The big coin machines are found only in larger casinos catering to more affluent players, while 10¢ and 50¢ machines are not as readily found, as they have given way to the proliferation of penny machines.

Multi-Denomination Machines

Multi-denomination machines allow you to play at various stakes by choosing the value of each credit you wager from the options listed on the machine. For example, one multi-denomination machine may allow you to bet quarters, dimes, nickels or pennies, while another may allow you to bet in denominations of 50¢, $1, $2 or $5. After you insert your bill or ticket, you select the denomination you wish to play and the slot machine automatically calculates the number of credits you will receive in exchange for the amount of money you inserted.

Converting Credits into Dollars

When you've finished playing and are ready to cash out, you'll need to make your way over to a machine that converts tickets into money or go to the cashier's cage. These conversion machines are clearly marked on the casino floor. They convert payout vouchers into money, change larger denomination bills into smaller denomination bills, and they are ATMs.

INSERTING MONEY

Modern Slot Machines

The slot machines on modern casino floors today only take paper money. Long, long gone are the old-fashioned machines that could be played with coins and that would noisily spit out the winning spins into the metal tray below. Winning spins today are marked by a variety of sound effects—the bigger the win, the more emphatic the noise. But that's not the only change brought about by modernization of the industry. The old term for slot machines, "one armed bandits," so named because the reels were activated by the handle on the side of the machine, is no longer apropos. For one, most players don't even use the handles anymore—that is, if the machine even has a handle! A simple press of the button does everything.

For another, where the reels stop is not a mechanical function as before, but is calculated by computer chips using random number generators. The function of the mechanical device that spins the reels now is only to display the result calculated by the computer, not to determine it. In fact, the modern slot machine is essentially a fancied up computer device. We've come a long way, baby! In the not too distant future, a new breed of slot machines won't even accept cash; they'll be playable only from a special slots card or credit card that contains credits for play.

Playing by Coin

Some casinos have an area with slot machines that accept coins for players who like to play in the time-honored tradition of dropping coins directly into the machine, a method not too far removed from the original pre-slots designs more than 100 years ago. These machines have a coin slot, called a coin entry or coin acceptor, where you insert your coins into the machine to initiate action.

Establishing Credits

There are two ways to establish credits at a machine. The basic way of building credits is by simply putting money in the machine. Once your money is in, you can play. You can immediately establish credits by inserting, for example, a $20 or $100 bill into the machine, or inserting a paper ticket that has cash value. These credits will register on the display of the machine marked "Credits."

The second way is to earn these credits through wins. After every win, the amount won is automatically credited to your total. This amount will be posted underneath the area marked "credits" on your machine.

For example, if you line up a combination that pays eighteen coins, the number "18" will be posted for your credits. If you already had fifty credits accrued, then the win of eighteen would be added to your fifty credits of accumulated wins for a new total of sixty-eight credits. You can play on these credits for as long as you have them, or cash out at any time by pressing the "TAKE WIN" button.

Pressing the TAKE WIN button will generate a ticket for the full amount of credits you have earned. You can take that ticket to a casino machine that converts tickets into cash, or to the cashier to cash out, or insert it into another machine that will recognize the credits and allow you to play just as if you had inserted cash. Slots were always easy to play, but with today's technology, it is easier than ever.

On the old classic machines, if more money was won than the machine could pay out, an attendant would come by to pay the rest, and would call a slots manager to authorize that payment. Usually, the maximum amount that the machine would pay for winners was posted right on the machine itself. It would also state that the attendant will pay the remainder. When that was the case—and if you still find casinos offering these classic machines—do NOT leave your machine if you hit a big winner because some one else may come in to claim your prize or start playing another game unaware there is a live jackpot sitting there waiting to get paid Always wait until the attendant arrives to give you your winnings.

> ## TIP
> Never, ever leave a machine that owes you money. Wait for the attendant to come by no matter how long it takes. You should as soon leave your wallet on a New York City street corner as walk away from a machine that's stacked with winning credits.

The Slots Handle

The traditional way of playing slots was to use the handle located at the side of the machine to spin the reels. The original idea of the handle, besides its basic mechanical function of spinning the reels, was to give players the feeling of controlling their destiny. There was action involved on the part of the player, and it was fun. Players felt like they participated, though in reality, for the average player, there was no skill involved in the way a handle was pulled. One pull was as good as any other. But try to tell that to a superstitious gambler (just about every player)!

I say "for the average player," because the casinos had to contend with occasional slots cheats who were able to control the destiny of the spins by using various methods and skills they had developed. Techniques such as slamming, walking the reels, and other methods were part of the slots cheat's arsenal.

Only a few slot machines today still have handles, primarily classic progressive machines whose handles are small appendages located on the right side of the machines. On these machines, players can activate the reels either by either pulling the handle or by pressing a button on the machine.

The vast majority of modern slots are button-only machines. Experienced slots players, some of whom like to camp out at their machines for countless hours at a time, like the fast action and easy play of the buttons. And casinos prefer that players use the faster method of playing by button (and by credits), since it generates more dollars played per hour and therefore, higher profits for them.

THE SLOTS ENVIRONMENT

You walk into the casino, hot cash in hand, and say to yourself, "I came to gamble!" The casino is buzzing with noise and excitement. Over by the craps table a Texan is screaming, "Eighter from Decatur!" You don't understand craps anyway. The blackjack tables are quieter, but don't look inviting, and roulette just isn't your style.

Forget all that. You came to play slots. Here's what the slots environment looks and feels like:

The Slots Setting

Slot machines dominate more floor space in casinos than any other gambling game. The slot machines make so much money for the casinos and generate so much action that a casino owner would have to be shortsighted or idiotic not to maximize the presence of these machines wherever possible. And really, how can you have a real casino without the general noise and ruckus created by the bells, whistles, sirens, catchy music, and screaming of slots players?

Slot machines are grouped together in blocks called banks. A bank of machines might consist of four machines grouped together in a square shape, with backs toward the middle and fronts facing outward toward the players, or even in larger groups of eight, ten, fifteen, or even more machines lined up in a row, or in circular or rectangular shapes.

Some banks of classic machines if you can still find them, are built around a platform. Formerly, in the old days—though you may find this relic of an operation in some small places— these machines were manned by a slots attendant whose job was to give the players change when needed, give encouragement, and keep the customers happy and playing. These configurations of slot machines are called carousels.

Within each bank there are a variety of machines. You may see three or more machines of one type from the same manufacturer next to a few from another within the same bank, or even alternating machines with no particular pattern you can discern.

The placement of machines is decided by the slots director or manager, who make these decisions based upon what he or she perceives to be the maximum effectiveness. Thus, it is quite normal to see a multitude of different styles within the same bank. A bank of slots will usually contain machines using the same coin denomination. It is unusual to see different denominations such as 25¢ and $1 machines mixed together within the same bank, but with multi-denomination machines, even that is changing.

For example, one bank will contain nothing but 25¢ machines, while a neighboring bank will contain only $1 slots. This type of arrangement makes it easier for customers to identify the type of machine they want, first by finding machines with the coin amount they want to play, then by choosing the style of machine they prefer. Also, players who switch machines or play two machines or more at a time can easily do so with the same coin value by remaining in the same bank.

Progressive slot machines are typically grouped together in the same block, and at the equal coin value, so that the posted sign showing the progressive jackpot above the machines can refer to all the machines within the group. Banks of progressives are common in a casino and great draws for players looking to make a lot of whoopee from a little whoopee.

It is compelling for slots players, just as it is for lotto players, to go for the dream of the ultimate killing, the jackpot of all jackpots, the outside hope that drives slots players to the machines in droves and keeps them playing. Slots players, as much as any other group, love the stories of the million and multi-million dollar winners. They can never hear enough of these get-rich-quick fantasies, as they're always thinking that it could happen to them. And it could—if they get lucky.

Slot machines get ever more colorful, fanciful, and boisterous, seemingly by the month. Brightly lit displays, garish colors, flashing lights, and rows of seated players pushing tickets into the machines make up the visuals of a slots area. Add to this the cacophony of sounds from the machines themselves and the periodic commotion caused by a gleeful winner, and you have the slots area.

Chairs

Each slot machine in the casino has a chair in front of it, so that you can play the machines in comfort, especially if you play for hours, which many players do.

SLOTS EMPLOYEES

The casino has a number of staff devoted to the slots area, and I'll go over their functions next.

Slots Attendants

Often called changepeople, the main job of these employees is to provide ready assistance to players. A secondary job of these front line slots people is to keep the player happy, whether through commiseration with a losing streak, exchanging small talk, or providing tips to a player requesting them.

Casinos are well aware that a moment's hesitation in assisting a player with the service they ask for could cause that player to get bored or annoyed and leave the area, so they employ enough slots attendants to keep their customers satisfied. Slots attendants who work in stationery positions in the high-stakes carousels often double as cheerleaders.

Believe me, when these changepeople root for you, they truly are rooting for you, because a happy winning player tends to tip, sometimes really well.

Slots Hosts

Most major casinos, and many smaller ones, hire employees specifically assigned to take care of slots players' needs. These employees, called slots hosts, usually can be summoned upon the player's request at the players club booth. (We'll talk more about players clubs later on in a chapter specifically devoted to this topic.)

The slots host spends most of his or her time working with players club members, helping players determine how much their credits are worth, processing special requests such as restaurant comps or show tickets, or dealing with other issues that come up. His or her job is to take good care of the slots players and make sure their experiences at the casino are as first rate as he or she can provide.

TIPPING

Tips, known as tokes in casino parlance, are expected in casinos, just as they are at the table games and similarly, at restaurants or bars. There are several employees you may want to tip. First of all, you have the servers who bring you drinks. It is customary to tip them every time they deliver a drink or round of drinks that you have ordered.

It is also customary at the machines to tip the slots attendant when you win big. For example, if you win several hundred dollars, or several thousand dollars, you may want to spread a little love around to the slots attendant that has helped you. As a rule of thumb, Las Vegas regulars tip one or two percent of their jackpot winnings. Gratuities are optional, of course, as it is with tipping anywhere—it is entirely up to you what you do with your money. If you really get lucky and win the jackpot, you may want to spread a lot of love around.

However, if you're losing or not winning much at the machines, you don't need to be giving out gratuities to the slots attendants—you've already donated enough to the casino's coffers. Tips usually aren't expected from losers, unless a slots attendant has given you incredible service.

TYPES OF SLOT MACHINES

In this chapter, I'll describe the various types of slot machines available for play, from the older style single-coin machines to the multi-coin machines, multipliers, progressives, Big Berthas, buy-your-play, wild symbol, multi-game, touch-screen, reel slot, and video slot machines.

CHOOSING A MACHINE

The first step in playing the slots is choosing the machine you wish to play. You'll find a multitude of slot machines of many different styles and from many different manufacturers in the casinos. Choosing the right machine, the one that you're most comfortable playing and best fits your needs, will be the first decision that you'll need to make. From there, you'll need to decide how many credits to play per line on the video slots. This is actually one of the most important decisions you'll make and one we'll discuss carefully in money management.

SINGLE CREDIT MACHINES

The single credit machines, a dying breed, used to be the only type of slots available to the player, that is, until the invention of the multiple-credit machine. Nowadays single-credit machines are rarely found, being much less profitable for the casino than a machine that takes one hundred credits or hundreds of credits. By the same token, the single-token slot appears dull and archaic compared to the modern video slots machine. They are off the casino floor in major casinos for a reason—no one wants to play them anymore when they have the choice of playing the new and exciting breed of slots.

Still, you may find single-credit machines in small, out-of-the way venues. Single-credit machines have that old-time feel, and are fun to play for players who love nostalgia. They're slower and clunkier than their modern cousins, and playing just one credit per spin will make your money last a little longer.

MULTIPLIERS

In 1967, Bally's introduced the 908 machine, the first slot machine to take multiple coins for play while giving winners increased proportional payouts for every coin played. These slots are known as multipliers. These innovative machines led the way to a new era in slots, which was great for both players and casino alike—everyone got a chance to have more action on each spin.

This evolution continues today, but no longer is it a multiplier machine accepting from one to five credits, with an occasional six-credit machine to be found as in a classic machines; video slot machines, in particular the penny slots, which dominate the market today, accept much larger numbers of credits for a single play. You can bet 10 credits per payline on many penny slots and as many as 100 paylines (sometimes more) can be triggered into action. Altogether, some machines can accommodate as many as 500 to 1,000 credits per play.

A multiplier works much like a single-credit machine, except that each credit deposited into the machine pays that much more proportionately than a single credit. Thus, two credits will pay twice a single credit for the same winning combination, three credits will pay three times, and five credits will pay five times. For example, if hitting three cherries pays two credits when a single credit is bet, three credits would yield a payout of six credits.

A multiplier of twenty credits on a penny machine, for example, would yield a 20-times payout. So if one credit wins five credits, one hundred credits would win five hundred credits.

Multipliers typically work proportionately on all wins, except for the biggest jackpot payoff, where a win for all credits played is sometimes much larger than if a lesser amount of credits were deposited. This incentive encourages you to bet the maximum number of credits the machine allows. On these types of payout structures, you should bet the maximum number of credits to take advantage of the bigger payouts.

MULTIPLE PAYLINE MACHINES

Much like bingo, multiple payline slot machines—which are all multiple-credit types of slots—give you multiple directions that can turn into a winner. The classic single payline machine has one line across the display that shows where the reels must line up for a winning combination to be paid. The classic multiple payline machine has three or five lines, depending upon the machine, which gives you more winning positions on the reels.

Video slot machines, on the other hand, have many more paylines, up to 100 on some games. That's a lot more excitement.

On multiple payline machines, each credit inserted activates a payline. On a three payout line classic machine, there are three horizontal lines. One line goes right across the middle as in a single payout line machine, a second line is above, and the third line below. To the left of each line, the display will be marked something like 1st credit payline for the center line, 2nd credit payline for the top line, and 3rd credit payline for the lower line. As each credit is inserted, the payline boxes light up indicating that they're in play.

Classic five-credit payline machines have two additional lines that crisscross the payout area diagonally. Appropriately, these machines are referred to as five-line criss-cross machines, or simply criss-cross machines. These machines have additional boxes indicating 4th credit payline and 5th credit pay-ine. These two indicators will light up when the fourth and fifth credits are inserted.

Winning spins can now be formed in any of the five directions on the five line machine, or on the three horizontals on the three-line machine.

The multitude of paylines on video slot machines are not as easily discernible. With slots that pay many lines, the machine cannot display all the information. However, the paylines that have been hit for winning combinations can be accessed by pushing the PAYOUT button.

BUY-YOUR-PAY MACHINES

These frustrating machines sometimes catch unwary players off guard and account for annoying headaches when a player who has seemingly scored a winning combination, or even a jackpot, finds out that not enough credits have been played and ends up winning nothing.

You can recognize the buy-your-pays by looking at the payout schedule on the face of the machine. They'll show the combinations of winners when one credit is played, a different group of winners when a second credit is played, and an additional group of winners for additional credits played on three and five credit classic buy-your-pay machines.

The buy-your-pay slots work on a different concept than the other machines you'll find. These classic machines have a single payout line and typically accept up to three or five credits.

They will only pay on certain symbols if enough credits are played. For example, the first credit might only credit cherries as the winner, but if another winner is hit, such as the bars or sevens, it won't pay because the requisite number of credits weren't inserted!

These classic machines are less prevalent now than previously, but since they can still be found, you'll need to be on guard if you find yourself playing them. When playing buy-your-pay machines, always play the maximum number of credits.

WILD PLAY MACHINES

Wild play machines give you a chance to double, triple or even quintuple (five times) your winning payout if a wild symbol lines up as part of their winning combination. And if two wild symbols line up as part of that combination, the winning payout will be multiplied by four times, nine times and twenty-five times respectively. When three wild symbols show, they are their own winning combination and are not multiplied by each other, as with two wild symbols. You'll see that combination listed on the front of the slots.

These classic wild play machines add a lot of excitement to the game, especially when they are hit. It's always fun to watch a winning combination take off when you hit one or two wild symbols.

IGT led the way with its very popular Double and Triple Diamond machines. The wild symbol on these machines is, of course, the diamond. When they were introduced, these machines were the most popular slot machines in the industry. You might also see machines on the floor with a five times multiplier. New machines are being developed and marketed all the time, so you'll have to keep your eyes open for other exciting concepts as well.

Just about all penny video reel machines have a wild play feature that increases the payouts and adds excitement to the game. When you hit a wild card symbol, it's really a lot of fun watching the credits pile up on your machine.

PROGRESSIVES

Progressive slot machines feature a growing jackpot that increases each time a credit is inserted into a machine that is hooked up to the progressive. When the jackpot hits, the lucky player wins the total money accumulated in the jackpot. At the same time, the jackpot total will be reset to a predetermined amount, ready to begin climbing again. Progressive jackpots can be relatively high if they've gone a while without hitting, or relatively low if they have been hit recently.

There are three types of progressives, which we will cover later, but the one that fields the biggest jackpots are linked together with a number of casinos. These inter-casino linked progressive slot machines draw tremendous amounts of excitement among players. The dream of hitting a one million dollar jackpot with one spin of the reels gets players excited. However, a one million dollar jackpot is a "small" jackpot nowadays. As more players get into these linked progressives, the jackpots are now in the millions. Jackpots as large as $5 million, $10 million, and even larger are being caught by lucky players these days.

Megabucks, Quartermania and Wheel of Fortune are examples of inter-casino linked progressives that accumulate enormous jackpots.

BIG BERTHAS

I can't write a slots book without mentioning the most classic slot machine of them all: the Big Bertha! The classic Big Bertha machines are gigantic slot machines with many reels, usually eight to ten, which are strategically placed by casinos near their front entrance. These novelty machines are always great eye-catchers and conversation pieces, and sometimes casinos will give you a free spin to lure you inside. While the payout percentage on Big Berthas isn't very high, and the machines are mostly played by tourists for a few spins, it is enjoyable for first-timers to spin the reels on the largest breed of slot machine in the world.

MULTI-GAME MACHINES

Multi-game slot machines are quite popular because you can switch from one game to another without having to change machines each time you want to change games. One multi-game mix may offer you the choice of playing video keno, video slots, video blackjack or video poker—all on the same monitor. These are very popular in bars where players are killing time drinking and get to choose among a few games to pass the time.

Multi-game machines often offer multi-denomination choices as well. For example, you might start off playing video keno in nickel denominations, and then switch your play to video blackjack for quarters by simply pressing a few buttons.

TOUCH-SCREEN MACHINES

Many modern machines don't even require that you press buttons. Instead, you touch the options you want to activate by simply pressing a finger on the appropriate symbol on the machine's video screen. Touch-screen machines, such as video keno and video poker, are quite popular, especially those that offer flat-top machines where the video monitor is embedded into a shelf that allows you to look down at the monitor and provides a place to rest your arms during play.

CLASSIC REEL SLOT MACHINES

The classic reel slot machines, which feature three reels or five reels (and sometimes as much as eight or ten reels, on novelty Big Bertha-type machines) have, for them most part, been replaced by the newest generation of slots, the video slot machines.

VIDEO SLOT MACHINES

Video slot machines have become the standard in modern casinos. Unlike the three to five paylines in reel slots, video slot machines may have 9, 15, 25, or even 100 different paylines. Video slot machines have no moving parts at all, as they are essentially computer games with graphic representations of reels that are spinning. In addition to the multitude of paylines that can form winning combinations, the video slot machines also offer bonus rounds—free spins that are activated by hitting combinations that trigger the bonus round.

Many video slot machines have a theme based on a popular TV game or show and feature vivid graphics and catchy music. Examples of video reel slot themes include Monopoly, Elvis Presley, and Love Boat.

10 SLOTS MYTHS DEBUNKED

I hear so many outrageous beliefs, falsehoods and outright misconceptions from gamblers, slots players, and casino employees about how slots really work and what is good luck and back luck on the machines, that I felt compelled to devote an entire chapter so you understand what is real in the world of slots, and what is just old wives tales and malarkey.

So much misinformation is passed around concerning slots and what it takes to win that most players are unable to separate truth from fiction anymore. If you hear enough of the same nonsense from enough people you might start to think it's credible. Unfortunately, there are not many good sources out there to hang your hat on, so understandably, it's difficult to find out what is real and what is fiction.

Well, let's start with this: The information in this chapter is factual. Anyone that has a different opinion out there—be it fellow slots player, slots manager, gambling author or expert—is wrong.

The worst misconceptions of all come from the people whom you might least expect—the employees who man the slots areas. I have talked to slots managers, floor people, attendants, and slots hosts, and not once did I hear fewer than two "facts" or ideas about slots from them that were flat-out wrong. I thought that if the people you would expect to be savvy, the ones working the slots areas every day, don't know the real deal, how could my readers possibly know?

From other slots players? Not quite.

So before I move on to the winning strategies in the next chapter, let me set the record straight on a number of points. Debunking these myths will not be refreshing for you, but profitable. Or at the very least, educational. Whatever you think you know about slot machines that you gathered from information given you from casino employees and other players, leave it all behind. The truth is on its way.

MYTH #1:
Slot Machines are the Worst Gamble at a Casino

There are plenty of worse gambles in the casino. Take a stroll down to the keno lounge or big wheel, make some of the high percentage bets at craps, make bonehead plays at blackjack, bet a parlay at the sports book. An average loose machine pays better than roulette and all of the above examples.

Next time a friend tells you how bad your odds are at the slots, hear a little more about what they play and the bets they make. You may be getting the better end of the bargain.

MYTH #2:
Pushing a Button or Pulling the Handle a Certain Way Will Make You a Winner

On the few machines that still have a handle, pulling it slowly, quickly, gently or roughly will not alter your probability of winning. Pushing the "spin reel" button in a particular manner as opposed to pulling the handle won't change your luck either. You win or lose depending upon how the luck goes, and the little twirls and shuffles you might do to get the winner going won't make a bit of difference.

This doesn't mean we're not all a little superstitious and will try every move to get the machines to cooperate. What I mean is, don't catch me with my own moves at the machines, I may get embarrassed. If I think standing on one leg is bringing me winners, I may be hopping like a bird. The reality, however, is that the machine can't see, feel or sense me hopping. And if it did, it might not understand what I was doing anyway.

If it could, the slots gods would be having a good laugh. Wouldn't stop me from hopping though if I was winning.

You can push a button with two fingers of your right hand trying to angle a play or the opposite fingers of your left hand influencing it in a different direction; press it with the gentlest touch or slam on it with your palm; whisper sweet things in its ear (wherever that may be) or yell at it; or do any of the millions of techniques players do to influence a winning combination at the slot machine.

But no matter what you do, it won't affect the odds or your chances of winning.

MYTH #3:
A Machine That Has Just Won Shouldn't Be Played Because It Won't Pay Out Again for the Longest Time

Just because someone won at a machine doesn't mean that you couldn't hit the jackpot again five minutes subsequent to that time. It is unlikely that you will hit the jackpot five minutes later, but no more unlikely than if you played the machine one month later, the slot machine next to it or the one across the street.

Slot machines have no such programming installed, and if they did, it would be classified as a cheating device. No casino is dumb enough to risk being shut down for this, and no casino needs to even consider this. The slots give them plenty of built-in profits.

If this myth were true, slot strategy would be simple. Avoid machines that just won, play machines that are overdue. But the fact is, it is just a myth.

MYTH #4:
A Machine That Hasn't Paid Out Recently is Ready to Hit

Myth #4 is a variation on Myth #3. The short rebuttal to the myth is that a cold machine isn't ever due for anything because there is no such programming installed on the machines.

Some players scour the casinos looking for machines that have been played for a long period of time without paying out. They believe that because a particular machine hasn't recently hit, it is due for a substantial payout. Again, the machines are set to be random for every spin of the reels. What occurred on the previous play has no bearing on the current play.

If you think a particular machine is ready to serve up a jackpot and you feel comfortable playing it, by all means give it a whirl. Just realize that your chances of winning at that machine are no better or worse than a similar machine that may have hit the day before.

There is only one part of the myth that is valid here and it is the opposite of what the myth suggests: If a machine is running really cold, it may be because it is set tighter than other similar machines. In that case, do the opposite of what the myth suggests—avoid the cold machine!

MYTH #5:
Slot Machine Managers Know When Certain Machines Are Due to Pay Out

Really? They know when machines are ready to spit out a jackpot as well as I know what the exact temperature and precipitation levels will be one month from now. If a slots manager knew a machine was about to spit out the sweet land of milk and honey, believe me, you wouldn't be the one playing that machine or even have a chance at it—you'd be watching his or her mother, spouse, or other family member or best friend camped out in front of it.

MYTH #6:
Machines Pay Less When a Players Club Card is in It

Casinos issue a players club card to their guests for the specific reason of tracking a player's action and rewarding them for their action. Good players get an array of perk—complementary meals, shows, hotel rooms, priority bookings and service, cash rebates, and much more.

The notion that casinos have set the circuitry of the machines to pay less when a slots card is inserted is unfounded. It would also be cheating. Casinos would risk far too much with the gaming board to play this kind of game to say nothing of the manufacturers of that machine. They already have their profits built-in, and certainly don't want to make the machines less attractive for their premier players.

If anything, the opposite might be true. Casinos have their slot machines set just the way they want them, slots card or not.

To reiterate, the sole purpose of the players club card is to tally the amount spent by the gambler. This in no way alters the inner workings of the game to pay out less to the player. The card is used only as a tracking device of a player's action, nothing more.

MYTH #7:
Machines Pay Less During Holidays and Big Events

Casinos make enough profits from the slot machines without having to change their payout probabilities on holidays. Casinos want winners, because winning begets action. I am not aware of any casino policy that alters the tightness or looseness of slot machines during crowded times.

Las Vegas, for example, is filled year-round with special events—boxing matches, large conventions, holidays, seasonal crowds, etc. Popular Indian casinos are often packed during weekends, holidays, and when they run certain promotions. But if this myth were true, these casinos would be so busy tightening or loosening their slots percentages that they would have a hard time getting anything else done.

MYTH #8:
You Will Win More at the $1 Machines

You also might lose more. As I will discuss in great detail later, the average higher denomination machines pay at a higher percentage than the average lower denomination machines, but the few percentage points aren't worth it if playing at that level is over your head. If you're looking strictly at percentage payouts, then this actually is true—higher denomination machines, on average, pay better than lower denomination machines. Hurrah, this is not entirely a myth, but you'd better read up on the money management discussions in this book before you bump up to playing bigger than you planned.

MYTH #9:
The Penny Machines are the Best Value on the Slots Floor

Huge myth! First of all, if you're defining value as cheapest to play, the penny slots are anything but a cheap play. Because people don't play them for just a penny. They play them for as much as twenty-five, fifty, one hundred credits or more to take advantage of all the paylines. If you're a penny player, you know what I'm talking about.

There is another way to define "best value" and that s by percentage payback. As we will discuss in the "Penny Slots" chapter, the penny machines are the absolute worst of the various denominations available to you.

Sorry penny players, that is the fact.

MYTH #10:
If I Play a Slot Machine With a 5% Edge, I Should Only Expect to Lose About $5 of My $100 Session Bankroll

Wring! Wrong! Wrong! The game or session has no idea whether you start with a $100 bankroll, $500 bankroll, or even a $1,000 bankroll. If your session was, say one hour, do you think the average loss would be the same? The answer is, it wouldn't, unless you played so much per pull that you lost your session bankroll. But let's say that didn't happen.

A 10% casino edge would suggest that you would lose $10 out of you $100, but ten times as much with the $1,000 starting bankroll, or $100. That's a substantial difference. If all bets were identical in value and you had the same results, how would that make sense? The answer is, it wouldn't. The disadvantage you are up against is only on the bets in play, not money kept on your person or deposited into the machine. That goes for all games, all bets, all play on every gamble. Your average loss is only a function of the action you give.

The percentage you might expect to win or lose is calculated on the total action you give the machine, that is, every spin times the amount bet. So if you play 200 spins in an hour and your average bet was 50 credits at a 1¢ machine (50¢ per spin), you would have played an average of $100 in that hour. At a 10% house edge, the long-term expectation is that you would lose $10 for that hour of play with a total of $100 in action. If you played for three hours, your long term expectation would be a loss of $30 (3 hours by $10 per hour), though anything can and often does happen in the short run.

So whatever table stakes you started with—$100, $1,000, or even $10,000—is irrelevant when figuring out what percentage or dollar loss or gain you might have when gambling.
But the myth is this: Your session bankroll has nothing to do with your percentage disadvantage to the house and the amount you would lose over the long run. Your win/loss expectation is solely dependent on the amount of action you give the casino.

THE NUMBERS: SLOTS PERCENTAGES

The unusual thing about slots, as opposed to the other casino games, is that you never know the exact payback percentages of a particular slots machine. Nowhere on the machine are the odds posted, nor can you determine from the type of machine, the manufacturer, or where the machine sits, what the payback will be. Even the slots personnel working the floor don't know what the house edge is on any particular slots machine.

You may see a casino advertise 98% or even 99% machines, but walk into the slots area and try to find those machines. There may be a few of them scattered around, but nowhere will there be a sign saying which machines they might be.

What do we know about payback percentages on the machines? First, let's go over just what is meant by "payback" and "house percentage." In this discussion, I'll be using both terms interchangeably. The payback is the amount the casino returns, on average, for every dollar placed into the machine. For example, if the casino advertises a 97% payback, they are telling you that for every hundred dollars invested into a machine, the expectation is that $97 of it will be returned.

In the long run, with hundreds of hours of plays, this is pretty much what will happen: you will lose $3 on average for every $100 played. That's the long run expectation. This $3 represents the house percentage or house edge, the mathematical amount a casinos can expect to win over a large number of trials. In gambling terms, it is also known as the casino's vigorish or vig.

In the short run, say a few hours or so of play, or even a dozen hours, anything can happen. Even though the casino has a vig of 3%, it wouldn't be unlikely for a player to be having a big day and be up hundreds on a quarter machine, or for some player to be hitting a jackpot worth thousands of dollars or much more. Even more likely, a player will be losing at the machine.

In other words, playing a machine with a 97% payback, your expectation is to lose $3 for every hundred dollars you gamble. This does not mean you will lose $3 for every hundred you bet. You may lose $20, or you may win $20. You may even hit the jackpot and be on easy street for the rest of your life. But in the long run, as many players challenge the machine and hour upon hour is invested into the machine, the return percentage will most likely approximate 97%. That machine will get its $3 per $100 played.

When you are playing against a house edge, it usually means you can expect to lose if enough hours are played.

THE ACTUAL HOUSE PERCENTAGES

The cut and dry fact at the slot machines is that the house has the advantage over the player, and the size of that advantage is strictly a function of the payback on the machines played. Paybacks on slots can vary from as little as 50% return on the dollar to as high as 99+% in rare cases.

Taking into account the benefits you can earn from the strategies I'll discuss in the "Players Clubs" and "21 Winning Strategies at Slots" chapters, you can have the edge sometimes. However, the norm is that the casinos maintain an edge at slots and build bigger, ritzier casinos from that edge.

In Atlantic City, the minimum payback is regulated by the state regulatory board, which requires that the slot machines have no less than an 83% return on the dollar, though if they did pay that little, few customers would play. In Nevada, the state gaming control board mandates that slot machines payback at least 75%, though practically speaking, casinos in Sin City pay back at a much higher rate than that.

Indian casinos are typically not legislated to maintain minimum payback percentages as Nevada and New Jersey casinos must do as required by their respective gaming control boards. So it's difficult to make a generalization on percentages in tribal casinos except to say that, like other casinos, if they want players to play slots in their facilities, they need an attractive payback percentage.

The Las Vegas casinos are in a very competitive market and compete heavily for patronage from the legions of slots players. This is good news for you, because it makes for more competitive rates, which means a higher percentage payback. Most casinos set their 25¢ and $1 machines for the mid-90% in payback. This is a high enough percentage to maintain a steady stream of money while at the same time allowing enough winners to keep everyone coming back for more.

Players react to ringing bells, flashing lights, and the whooping and hollering of winning players—all the signs that a slots player is winning. These sounds generate excitement throughout the immediate area and get everybody thinking about playing those machines. Everyone wants to win.

Casinos that set their machines in the mid 90% range generate a lot of noise, and thus a lot of play. That's why many of the Las Vegas casinos do so well at the slots. You'll find a lot of slots players, regular patrons and first timers, who get drawn into the slots action. Excitement begets action. Within these slots areas will be machines set at lower percentages for higher profit margins, but overall, the best way for casinos to make money is to make sure there are enough winners. That is why you'll find good and bad paying machines interspersed among one another.

There are also casinos whose top machines will pay in the 80% range, perhaps lower. While these casinos will make a higher percentage of money per machine, they won't make anywhere near the gross amount of profit that a more savvy casino paying a higher percentage payback to the customer might make. Players quickly realize when they're at a machine that's not very encouraging. It doesn't take a rocket scientist to see that one is having less fun at a machine because of fewer payoffs.

Locals will migrate to where their luck is better and tourists will be drawn to machines where the excitement level is higher. Word of mouth will also spread among players. They might say, "Avoid this place, the slot machines are like a morgue," or "Play here, I was killing the machines." Sure, poorer paying machines will always have their customers, but not at the same intensity level or length of time played as in a casino that has set the mood for winning.

PLAYERS CLUBS

Players clubs are the best way for slots players to amass a seemingly endless parade of room comps, meal comps, show comps, line passes, and even cash rebates. In fact, if you play your reels right, you can virtually enjoy free vacations doing just what you like to do best in the casinos—playing the slots! And that's not bad at all.

Why all the fuss?

Given the large amount of profits that casinos earn from their slots players, and their recognition of the importance of the revenue they generate, you, as a slots player today, are king or queen. No longer are the table games the real bread and butter of a casino. This is not the '70s anymore. It's the new era of the slot machines where they comprise more than 50% of a typical casino's action.

Casinos rely more and more on their slots players to generate bottom-line profits and have steadily increased the space allocated to slots to reflect this. Now, anywhere you go in a modern casino, you see them, you hear them, you feel them. The slot machines are expanding throughout casinos like some blob out of a '60s era flick. As fast as their presence expands, new players expand with them, plopping the credits into the bellies of the beasts.

Slots players are no longer taken for granted. With slots revenues in the billions worldwide, casinos are realizing who their important players really are and are actively pursuing their patronage. Comps, incentives, and bonuses, once reserved for table players, are now in the full domain of the slots player.

That's great news for slots players because casinos are motivated to get you to their machines rather than their competitors' machines, a situation I'll show you how to take advantage of for your full benefit.

ABOUT THE PLAYERS CLUBS

Players clubs are enrollment programs that you sign up for as members of a casino's slot club. There is no charge to become a member, but lots of benefits. The concept is simple. Once you're enrolled, the casino will issue a member card with your name and card number. These cards are inserted into the machines prior to play and automatically track your betting action. The more action you give the casino, the greater the benefits you enjoy just for playing the machines you were going to play anyway. That's a benefit for you.

For example, in casinos that aggressively cater to slots players, after approximately just one hour of action at the $1 machines, or two to three hours at the quarter machines, you might be able to accrue enough credits to qualify for the lowest level of benefits. The benefits and comps you can earn are all a function of the amount of money played. And that, in casino parlance, is called action. Action, to a casino, is not some theoretical concept—it's the total amount of money played.

For example if you're playing 1¢ slots, one hundred credits at a time, and play 1,500 spins, you've given the casino $1,500 worth of action, 1,500 spins by $1 each. If you're playing quarters, five at a time to a machine, and play 1,000 spins, your action is equal to 5,000 quarters, or $1,250.

Note that the action given to a machine or a casino is not measured by how much you've won or lost, but the total amount of plays multiplied by the amount bet. Thus, using the above example at the $1 machines, whether you've won $115 overall, or lost $115, your action is still that same $1,500 from the casino's point of view. Plenty good to start earning comps, and really good now that you've earned a $115 profit to show as well.

UNDERSTANDING "ACTION"

Note that the action given to a machine or a casino is not measured by how much you've won or lost, but the *total amount* of plays multiplied by the amount bet.

And that's why players clubs are so great. If you're going to be playing the machines, you're guaranteed "winnings," so to speak, by dint of the simple fact that your action is earning rewards. For example, if you're playing the penny slots and drop $23 at the machines after many hours of play, but earn two free buffet comps along the way, you're not feeling so bad. You've come out ahead of the game.

These players cards are great tracking devices that not only record your total action and the total amount of money wagered at the machine, but keep track of your behavior so that the casinos can better understand the machines you like to play, in what denominations, and how long each machine is played. It allows them to better market promotions to you.

Each casino has its own players clubs program, some with greater benefits than others. But all are worth joining if you plan to play slots at a casino, and especially if you plan on playing a lot of slots. Each casino has a special name for its players club: for example, Caesars Player's Club is called Total Rewards, Station Casinos club is named Boarding Pass. Further, your players club card is valid at all of a casino's properties. For example, you can use the same players club card at any of the properties owned by Harrahs. Ditto for Mandalay Resorts, Park Place Entertainment, Stations casinos in Las Vegas, and Boyd Gaming properties in Las Vegas.

Player's Clubs began as an experiment at the Sands Casino in Atlantic City in 1982 as a method to attract and keep slots players in their casino. In 1984, the Golden Nugget introduced this concept to Las Vegas and, as they say, the rest is history. Almost every casino today in Las Vegas or Atlantic City has an actively promoted players clubs. Any that don't are at a tremendous marketing disadvantage. After all, why would a serious slots player patronize a casino offering nothing special to attract his or her play when the casino next door has a great players club with tons of inducements? The answer is simple: They wouldn't.

While the casinos are eager to induce players into their casinos with attractive players club benefits, players are just as eager to reap the rewards. The trick is learning how to play the system for the full amount of the awards.

SHOULD YOU JOIN A PLAYERS CLUB?

Absolutely! If you're going to be playing the slots, you should definitely join. You have nothing to lose and everything to gain. The application requires nothing more than your basic information; the membership has nothing to do with income level or credit information. Outside of the few minutes it might take to apply, there is no other effort needed to enjoy the many benefits.

Some players think that they don't gamble enough to even bother signing up. Au contraire. It's not how much you're willing to risk at the machines, it's the amount of action you give those machines that counts. Well, you might say, I'm only going to play with $100. That $100 may earn you $50, $100, or more in benefits if your luck is good.

Let's say you get on a roll at the penny slots and everything goes your way. You win a bunch, lose some back, and go back and forth in your play. When all is said and done, many hours later you walk away with a small $22 profit. Or, let's just say that the machine swallowed up that $22. Either way, you've possibly generated enough action to receive some benefits. In total, if you add up all the bets you made during that playing session it might add up to thousands of dollars in action.

That's a lot more significant than the mere $100 you thought you were wagering. Many players don't realize this and lose out on benefits they otherwise could have accumulated.

GETTING STARTED

Joining a players club is as easy as filling out an application form. Modern casinos have special areas, generally called Club Booths, where specially trained employees assist customers who want to sign up for the casino's players club.

The application process for joining is simple and the application itself won't take long to fill out. The casinos are mostly concerned that they can properly identify you and that they can get you on their mailing list to keep you abreast of the latest and most exciting developments from their players club. There is no charge to join a players club—it is always free.

Keep in mind that this application is simply a formality—nobody is going to get turned down. They have no interest in your credit history or how much money you make. This is not a credit application, only an application to initiate membership and entice you to play slots in their casino.

CHOOSING THE BEST PLAYERS CLUBS

In the beginning, getting the most for your gambling buck is a matter of researching the various casinos you're interested in and finding out who has the most generous incentives. Many casinos will give you a printed schedule showing how the rewards work. Comparing the different programs for their benefits is the best way to decide what's right for you. But this is the information, the legwork so to speak, you'll need to do as you're getting established among the various clubs.

Some casinos won't give you any information at all, and in fact, will claim they don't know the structure of their point system. These casinos should be avoided.

The real way to get going with the players clubs and reap the maximum benefits is to join them all, or at least as many as is practical! This doesn't mean you have to play in all of them. You should focus your playing in the casinos with the best machines and the best rewards. The others can lie dormant until the time is right. Meanwhile, you'll be on all the players clubs' mailing lists, and when there is a great slots promotion, you'll be in the know. These casinos know that they have a lot of competition and they want to get you in their door. That means they need to give you incentives for you to make your next trip to their casino. For that to work they have to give you an offer to seriously consider.

With offers galore coming in, you can start cherry-picking the best deals. Then you're on your way to all the freebies the casinos have to offer. With some good timing and a little luck, you may even build up enough points to earn yourself with a free vacation—rooms, meals, shows, cash rebates, and even more points built up for more comps.

GETTING STARTED ON THE COMPS

As soon as you sign up for a players club, casinos usually offer you freebies and incentives as your sign-up bonus. This could include meal or show discounts or comps, tee shirts, free play—really anything at all the casino is using as a promotion to get you to sign up for its club. These incentives frequently change depending on the promotions department.

The first thing that happens when you sign up for a players club is that you are issued a card. This card identifies you as a player and a member of the players club that issued it. You card is used to track your play at the machines. The casinos will have you on file and in the system. Armed with this card, you'll earn rewards credits every time you play. And if you tire of playing the machines and decide to play some live poker or make a sports wager, you'll earn credits at those games, too.

You will also need to select a pin number to be assigned to your player's card. Thereafter, whenever you enter the casino and before you begin playing your favorite slots, you will want to swipe your card, just like you'd swipe your ATM card at the mall to pay for a purchase, at one of the large, specially designated players club machines on the casino floor.

Most modern Las Vegas casinos require that you swipe your player's card in order to receive the promotions you are eligible for that day. The machine will ask you to punch in your pin number, which will trigger the promotions available to you. For example, if you are eligible to receive double points for your play that day, that option will appear on the screen. You then push a button to accept the offer.

Warning: If you do not register your player's card before you begin play, you will not receive the promotions you are eligible for.

Step one to ensuring at least some promotional offers is to put that card to use right away with a little action in the casino. This lets them know that they have a "live" player, and will make them work that much harder to ply you with incentives.

Some players clubs may want to qualify their players, that is, make sure you're really a player, one who is going to give them action and has proven so by already playing—not just someone who shows up on any list that he can get on. Or, perhaps casinos may give the qualified player better offers. In any case, players clubs change their offers all the time, depending upon their marketing programs, but I find that giving the card at least a little play is the safest way to get the ball rolling.

The next step toward really qualifying you as a player is to meet the casino's minimum level of play toward their first qualifying level of play. Again, the minimum playing requirements vary from casino to casino, and can vary from one month to another as policies and the competitive environment changes. You'll have to see where things stand if you've been away from the casinos for a while, and see if what was a good program the last time is still good, or if you perhaps find a players club you like even better for this trip.

Casinos that really value you as a customer will let you know up front what they expect from you. Just how much action you need to generate for the awards programs to kick in will be spelled out in black and white.

Typically, and again this varies completely from one program to another, approximately one hour worth of action at the $1 slots or the equivalent amount of action from the penny machines, or two to three hours at the 25¢ machines will kick in the first tier of bonuses. Some players may reach these levels a little faster if they play faster, slower players may take a little longer. Again, the critical element the casinos are looking for is the amount of action, how much money is wagered into the machines, not how long you happen to be sitting in front of a machine warming a chair.

The casinos want action. You give it to them, and they'll kick in with their incentives.

HOW THE SLOTS CARD WORKS

The most important factor in earning your full playing credits at the slot machines is to use your players club card. Every slot machine in the casino has a card reader that will accept your card. These are typically found in the front of the machines. If for some reason you can't find the reader, have trouble insert-ing your card into it, or have any other problem, call over one of the slots personnel. They'll be glad to help you get set up. That is what they are there for.

Upon approaching a machine and readying yourself for play, your first move is to insert your card into the card reader. Upon insertion, the card will usually identify you by name, though sometimes the casino will have a theme greeting instead.

WHAT IF YOU LOSE YOUR CARD?

If you've left your card back home or in your casino room or have even lost it altogether, no problem. Go to the players club booth and they'll give you a replace-ment card upon presentation of your ID. Lost cards are a regular occurrence at the casinos. Casinos will be happy to set you up again with your card and get you back into action.

EARNING THE FIRST LEVEL OF PLAYERS CLUB BENEFITS

Once you know the minimal levels of play you need to meet to qualify for the program's first level of benefits, the only variables that affect the time it takes to get to that first benefit level are the speed of play (how many spins on average you play per hour), the denomination you're playing, and the average number of credits you play per spin. The more money per hour you play, the faster you accumulate the action required by a casino to reach activation levels.

How do the casinos determine this first level? First you must understand how casinos rate a player's slots action in general, and then how they reward that action.

Casinos generally rate a player's action on a point system, awarding a certain number of points for each level of dollars played. You may receive one point per dollar played, one point per $20 played, or even ten points per $1 played. But none of this means anything unless you know what these points mean. Each point earned is relative to the value given to it by that particular casino.

TIP FOR EARNING EXTRA POINTS

You can earn action points at more than just slot machines. Your players club card is also good for racking up points at the video poker machines and at all the other machines in the casino. Many casinos also give you credits at the table games and sports book.

Each casino has its own point system and activation levels, and it is only by knowing these levels that you can make sense of which slots program is good, and which one is not quite as attractive. For example, getting ten points for $1 won't mean anything if the activation level for that casino requires you to spend twice as much time playing your preferred denomination machine as another casino. In other words, 1,000 points at one casino may be of more value to you than 1,000 points at a different one, and may even be of more value than 10,000 points at another casino that throws points around like Italian lira.

There are other ways that casinos rate a player's action at the slots, such as time played, but typically speaking, casinos will use the total dollar value action wagered by the player. The total number of credits placed into the machines multiplied by their dollar value is the most accurate and fair measure of play anyway. Playing three dollars a spin and spinning the reels 300 times yields an exact amount of action—$900. Another player may spend just as much time at that machine, and bet that same $3 per spin, but put in only one third as much play. Obviously, the first player is more valuable to the casino, and is a player they wan to reward with slot club benefits more than the second less-active player.

Casinos don't want to reward players just for time spent idling at a machine, players who perhaps just sit there soaking in the free drinks and the atmosphere and accruing points with little play. Casinos want action, and there is no better measure of that action than adding up the credits played.

POINT EXPIRATION

Your points can expire if you haven't returned to a casino within twelve months of your last visit. You'll have to ask your slots host if this applies to you. If so, make sure to redeem any awards before expiration.

Te following pages contain Action Charts that show the amount of time you have to play at different denomination machines to accrue different amounts of play at a casino.

PENNY SLOTS AND ACTION CHARTS

On penny slots, where you are playing multiple credits on each spin, just substitute the total credits played for the amount in the "Credit" column.

For example, if you bet an average of 25 credits per spin, which is 25¢, just match it up with the 25¢ row, and similarly, if you're averaging 100 credits per spin, use the $1 column to determine how many hours you need to accumulate $1,000 in play.

ACTION CHART—$1,000

Credit	Credits Played	Speed of Play Fast	Slow
5¢	5	10 hours	11 hours
	3	16 hours	18 hours
	1	50 hours	60 hours
25¢	5	2 hours	2.5 hours
	3	3.5 hours	4 hours
	1	10 hours	12 hours
$1	5	30 minutes	45 minutes
	3	45 minutes	1 hour
	1	2.5 hours	3 hours
$5	5	6 minutes	7 minutes
	3	9 minutes	11 minutes
	1	30 minutes	37 minutes

This chart shows approximately how long it would take to reach $1,000 in action. It does not takes into account the house payback (return percentage) since it is only tracking the number of bets multiplied by the size of the bet. Keep in mind that this chart is only an approximation, and that every individual's speed is different.

You see by the chart, that the fewer credits played per pull, the longer it takes to reach the level shown. Similarly, the slower the player's average playing speed, the longer it will take.

Since the average player will play the full amount of credits allowed by the machine, and the experienced player tends to go at faster paces, you can expect that the action levels will be hit more often at the faster pace.

ACTION CHART—$2,000

Credit	Credits Played	Speed of Play	
		Fast	Slow
5¢	5	20 hours	22.5 hours
	3	32.5 hours	37.5 hours
	1	100 hours	120 hours
25¢	5	4 hours	4.5 hours
	3	6.5 hours	7.5 hours
	1	20 hours	24 hours
$1	5	1 hour	1.5 hours
	3	1.5 hours	2 hours
	1	5 hours	6 hours
$5	5	12 minutes	14 minutes
	3	19 minutes	22 minutes
	1	1 hour	1.25 hours

This chart shows approximately how long it would take to reach $2,000 in action. It does not take into account the house payback (return percentage) since it is only tracking the number of bets multiplied by the size of the bet. Keep in mind that this chart is only an approximation, and that every individual's speed is different.

You see by the chart that the fewer credits played per pull, the longer it takes to reach the level shown. Similarly, the slower the player's average playing speed, the longer it will take.

Since the average player will play the full amount of credits allowed by the machine, and the experienced player tends to go at faster paces, you can expect that the action levels will be hit more often at the faster pace.

ACTION CHART—$3,000

Credit	Credits Played	Speed of Play	
		Fast	Slow
5¢	5	30 hours	34 hours
	3	48 hours	57 hours
	1	150 hours	180 hours
25¢	5	6 hours	7 hours
	3	9 hours	11.5 hours
	1	30 hours	36 hours
$1	5	1.5 hour	2.25 hours
	3	2.25 hours	3 hours
	1	7.5 hours	9 hours
$5	5	18 minutes	21 minutes
	3	28 minutes	33 minutes
	1	1.5 hours	2 hours

This chart shows approximately how long it would take to reach $3,000 in action. It does not take into account the house payback (return percentage) since it is only tracking the number of bets multiplied by the size of the bet. Keep in mind that this chart is only an approximation, and that every individual's speed is different.

You see by the chart that the fewer credits played per pull, the longer it takes to reach the level shown. Similarly, the slower the player's average playing speed, the longer it will take.

Since the average player will play the full amount of credits allowed by the machine, and the experienced player tends to go at faster paces, you can expect that the action levels will be hit more often at the faster pace.

ACTION CHART—$4,000

Credit	Credits Played	Speed of Play	
		Fast	**Slow**
5¢	5	40 hours	45 hours
	3	65 hours	75 hours
	1	200 hours	240 hours
25¢	5	8 hours	9 hours
	3	13 hours	15 hours
	1	40 hours	48 hours
$1	5	2 hours	3 hours
	3	3 hours	4 hours
	1	10 hours	12 hours
$5	5	24 minutes	28 minutes
	3	38 minutes	44 minutes
	1	2 hours	2.5 hours

This chart shows approximately how long it would take to reach $4,000 in action. It does not take into account the house payback (return percentage) since it is only tracking the number of bets multiplied by the size of the bet. Keep in mind that this chart is only an approximation, and that every individual's speed is different.

You see by the chart that the fewer credits played per pull, the longer it takes to reach the level shown. Similarly, the slower the player's average playing speed, the longer it will take.

Since the average player will play the full amount of credits allowed by the machine, and the experienced player tends to go at faster paces, you can expect that the action levels will be hit more often at the faster pace.

ACTION CHART—$5,000

		Speed of Play	
Credit	**Credits Played**	**Fast**	**Slow**
5¢	5	50 hours	56 hours
	3	81 hours	94 hours
	1	250 hours	300 hours
25¢	5	10 hours	11.5 hours
	3	16.5 hours	19 hours
	1	50 hours	60 hours
$1	5	2.5 hour	4 hours
	3	4 hours	5 hours
	1	12.5 hours	15 hours
$5	5	30 minutes	35 minutes
	3	46 minutes	55 minutes
	1	2.5 hours	3 hours

This chart shows approximately how long it would take to reach $5,000 in action. It does not take into account the house payback (return percentage) since it is only tracking the number of bets multiplied by the size of the bet. Keep in mind that this chart is only an approximation, and that every individual's speed is different.

You see by the chart that the fewer credits played per pull, the longer it takes to reach the level shown. Similarly, the slower the player's average playing speed, the longer it will take.

Since the average player will play the full amount of credits allowed by the machine, and the experienced player tends to go at faster paces, you can expect that the action levels will be hit more often at the faster pace.

ACTION CHART—$10,000

		Speed of Play	
Credit	Credits Played	Fast	Slow
5¢	5	100 hours	115 hours
	3	165 hours	190 hours
	1	500 hours	600 hours
25¢	5	20 hours	23 hours
	3	33 hours	38 hours
	1	100 hours	120 hours
$1	5	5 hours	7.5 hours
	3	7.5 hours	10 hours
	1	25 hours	30 hours
$5	5	1 hour	1.25 hours
	3	1.5 hours	2 hours
	1	5 hours	6.25 hours

This chart shows approximately how long it would take to reach $10,000 in action. It does not take into account the house payback (return percentage) since it is only tracking the number of bets multiplied by the size of the bet. Keep in mind that this chart is only an approximation, and that every individual's speed is different.

You see by the chart that the fewer credits played per pull, the longer it takes to reach the level shown. Similarly, the slower the player's average playing speed, the longer it will take.

Since the average player will play the full amount of credits allowed by the machine, and the experienced player tends to go at faster paces, you can expect that the action levels will be hit more often at the faster pace.

PLANNING AHEAD

Remember to prepare for your next trip to Las Vegas, or wherever you might be gambling, by contacting the players club at the casinos where you might be playing in order to get yourself set up in advance. Most casinos have toll-free 800 numbers, and will be glad to provide you with all the information you need to either sign up for their slots club or reap its benefits.

Of course, you can always sign up when you arrive, and that's no problem. But by alerting the casino that you're coming, or might be coming, they might send you incentives and comp tickets that might sweeten your trip.

PENNY SLOTS

Penny slots are the most played slot machines today. With the new generations of the video slots featuring cutting edge graphics, colorful animated themes, great sound effects, and clever game play, it is hard for slot players not to love all the bells and whistles of the new generation machines. Popular themes of these penny slots include TV shows like Wheel of Fortune and Love Boat, movies such as The Godfather, Avengers, Iron Man and Star Wars, and board games like Monopoly, and Yahtze,

But there is a thinly veiled price to playing the penny slots you'll find on casino floors today—the amount of playing time you receive compared to machines of yesteryear. A $100 of play today is nothing like $100 worth of play you got in the 1990s or even the early 2000s

The question penny slots players today must consider: How long will my fun last?

You can't even think of playing max credits with just a $20 bill at penny slots. Without a good run to start your session, you'll be gone before your drink order even gets placed. You need at least $100 to last a while, but even then, if you get too aggressive, you still might not last long enough for the server to bring your free drinks.

There is a lot of buzz and a lot of play in these machines, and I know that people love playing penny slots—but if you keep falling into the fallacy that they are "just penny machines," you will continue losing at a faster rate than ever before. I am not just talking about the average bet size, which is well over 50 pennies for most players, or even over 100 pennies for many others.

My concern is the casino's edge. It is enormous, double ad sometimes triple what can be found on other machines lining the casino floor. In fact, given the speed of play, the high amount of the average bet, and the enormous edge enjoyed by the casino, in terms of how far your money will last, the penny slots now rate as one of the worst gambles in the casino!

Here's why.

THREE REASONS THE PENNY SLOTS WILL QUICKLY DRAIN YOUR MONEY

1. Bad Percentages

Let's start with this: The casino has more than a 10% edge over you on the average penny slots machine, actually closer to 12% on the Las Vegas Strip! That is more than a lot; it is unsustainable as a player. This casino edge on penny slot machines is well more than double that of any many other types of slots you can play.

Look at the average percentage return on penny slots compared to other denominations in the greater Las Vegas area.

PENNY SLOT PERCENTAGES Las Vegas Area, 2014 to 2015		
	1¢ Machine	$1 Machine
Las Vegas Strip	88.24%	93.69%
Downtown	88.72%	95.24%
Boulder Strip	90.24%	95.66%
North Las Vegas	90.56%	96.12%

Note that these are averages and some machines will pay better than this and some worse. (Yes, some will be even worse!)

The chart shows that you will lose at twice the speed playing penny slots than $1 machines. But it's actually worse than that if you compare it to older generation machines with similar paybacks on the $1 machines. You'll lose at a faster rate than the percentages suggest for these additional reasons:

2. Speed of Play

Today's slot machines are fast. In the old days slot machines were designed with features to afford more game play. That is, they were designed to play more slowly. Today, that concept has disappeared somewhat in favor of machines having more repetitions per hour. That means your money gets played faster—and lost faster.

3. You're Not Really at a Penny Machine

You're not even at a nickel or even a quarter machine. Some machines require you to play a minimum of thirty lines; at 1¢ per line, so you're starting at a 30¢ minimum bet. It's easy to put mulitpliers on your bet, which can easily hike your spin up to several dollars. On some machines, you can even go as high as $10 per spin. Remember, these are penny machines, or at least the casino would like you to think they are.

If the video game has fifty paylines and you can bet twenty pennies per payline, for example, the machine can gobble up $10 per spin.

THE SKINNY ON PENNY SLOTS

How this plays out is something you'll quickly notice—the length of time it takes for your money to go. The bottom line is that you get much less playing time, or satisfaction as judged by amount of time played, out of today's penny slots than you did in the early 2000s and before. Your money just doesn't last. The casino's hold on slot machines is way up, over 40% in most places, but their actual profit is down. Gee, I wonder why.

The higher the casino edge, the faster, on average, your money will disappear. Long-term players rue the days when $100 or a few hundred dollars would stretch all evening. They got a lot of bang for their buck. They also won more often. That made for more excitement and enjoyment. Customer satisfaction is something the greedy casinos haven't figured out. Their slots handles have dropped considerably over the past bunch of years, all this at the same time that their average percentage advantage has soared.

An anomaly? An irony?

Nope, neither one. Players that win want to come back and win more. Players that have fun want to have more fun. But players who have their money fleeced so fast they barely had time to warm a chair don't have fun. They get discouraged, especially when their reload of money disappears real fast again.

What?

That's what happens when you're playing a very fast game, playing a bunch of coins at one time, and....the casino fleeces you on a rate of more than 10% per pull.

It is also true that the entertainment value of the penny slots is high. All the action, the lights, the noises, the themes—they all add up to a lot of fun, or at least a good diversion from reality.

If you love penny slots and you're there just to dump your money fast to play these machines, at least I have educated you. If lasting longer playing slots and giving yourself a better chance of winning are important, stay clear of the penny slots and go back to the traditional 5¢, 25¢ or $1 machines. You are better off playing a single $1 coin in a dollar machine than 100 credits (also $1) in a penny machine, often to the tune of 250% better!

Let's put that in perspective. If your money lasts an average of just one hour at the penny machines, you would have staying power of two-and-a-half hours at a standard $1 slots. Ninety minutes at a penny machine would translate to three hours and forty-five minutes. That's a huge difference. To put it another way, you can go on a run at a 25¢ or $1 machine and have a way better chance of having a winning session than at a penny machine, which gives you such a poor chance of winning that you will rarely walk away a winner.

Sound familiar?

WIDE-AREA PROGRESSIVES

There is one aspect concerning frequency of wins at wide-area progressive (WAP) slot machines—progressive machines linked together across many casinos such that the jackpots rise to high levels, such as Quartermania and Megabucks—that you need to understand to increase your winning chances. Not all 95% payback machines give you an equal chance of winning, nor do all 90% payback machines.

Huh? Don't 95% and 95%, and 90% and 90% equal one another? Yes and no. It depends upon how the cut has been apportioned to get those figures.

When all is said and done, that is, over the long run, two 90% machines will pay out equally and your chances of winning are equal. But the "long run" with WAPs is gauged by millions and millions of spins, so many spins that just a handful of players of the many million playing win that monster prize. The rest, eaten up by that longshot prize, suffer with fewer and shorter wins.

I'll explain this concept using three theoretical slot machines as an example. Let's say that you have $10 million in bets and there is a pool of $9 million in prizes. That makes these slots 90% payback machines. One hundred thousand people are playing the game, and on average, play 100 spins at $1 each, for a total bet of $100 per player. $100 multiplied by 100,000 players equals $10 million in bets.

We'll assume that the law of averages perfectly plays out so that the end result sees players taking back $9 million in prizes out of the $10 million bet for an average loss of 10%, that is, $10 per player. This aligns perfectly with the expected win rate. The casino will win their 10% and show a $1 million profit on these machines. That will be their hold.

What will be interesting is that the following three 90% payback machines will yield the same total for the casino no matter how the cake is cut. The difference is simply how the pie is divided. (From cakes to pies, you can see that I'm getting closer to the comp buffet.)

Let's now look at the three different machines to see how they affects your winning chances—the Mega-Machine, the Roll'Em Winner, and the Small Potato. Note that the Mega-Machine and Small Potato machines are not based on actual machines, but are used as extremes to illustrate the importance of a payback schedule. The Roll'em Winner approximates actual machines you'll find today.

MACHINE ONE: MEGA-MACHINE

The mythical Mega-Machine offers the winning player an $8 million jackpot when it is hit. This lucky winner will be set for life and will be one very happy camper. The $8 million paid out over twenty years comes out to a $400,000 per year check (less the IRS cut)—or, to put it another way, a financial dream come true. The hope of being this lucky winner and all the stories of other big winners keeps this type of machine hopping.

For one player, this is a dream come true. For the other 99,999 players, it leaves a slim pool of money to win and, consequently, big losses spread out among them, the ones who weren't fortunate to be the "one."

The other $1 million in the pool will be split up in winnings, on average, by all 100,000 players. One million dollars split up among 100,000 players comes out to an average return of $10 each. This means that on this machine, the average player will win back only $10 of the $100 played. Ouch! That's only a 10% average payback for all the other chumps, all 99,999 of them! Losing $90 out of every $100 wagered is highway robbery. So while the machine has a 90% payback, the average player will get only a 10% payback. That's horrendous!

Some players will do better and some will do even worse than the 10%. With such a small pool of other players winning money, very few winners emerge. It is really just one big unhappy pool of losers. Compare this to the 90% payback you thought you would see!

Who would want to play this machine? Note that this example is an extreme and no sensible casino owner would carry a progressive slot machine that returned so much to one player and so little to the rest. If they did, the players would quickly see that this game was virtually unplayable. Players would get little to no satisfaction out of the Mega-Machine progressive.

MACHINE TWO: ROLL 'EM WINNER

The Roll'em Winner is a lot more sane and gets a lot more action. It will average fifty $10,000 winners, and spread out the remainder of the $8,500,000 in winning spins over an assortment of different combinations.

Where winning spins on the Mega-Machine were few and far between, the Roll 'em Winner is chugging out payouts left and right. While the Roll 'em Winner machine doesn't put anyone on easy street, it also doesn't restrict itself to just one Lucky Louie. Now you have 50 eager beavers that bagged $10,000 in winnings on just one spin (plus whatever they accumulated on the other spins), which adds up to a lot more people returning from their trips with stories of the big hit.

And for the casino's benefit, fifty very happy players are telling everyone they know about how much fun they had and getting all their friends and family psyched for their own trips to the casinos.

The other $8,500,000 in payouts is spread out among the full assortment of 100,000 players (including the 50 big winners), to the tune of $85 per player. That averages out to an 85% return on the $100 bet. Again, some will win more on average and some will win less. But there will be a lot of winners after the 100 spins. Most players here will see some winning action and will have enjoyed themselves much more than the Mega-Machine players who pulled the handle in about as barren a winning desert as you can find.

MACHINE THREE: SMALL POTATOES

This fictional slot is designed to provide constant reinforcement to its players by enticing them with lots of small wins. Out of every ten spins, on average, six will pay back winners. The wins are small and little to get excited about, but they're wins nonetheless. One win out of ten wins will pay three credits per credit played, one will pay two credits per credit played, and four will pay one credit per credit played.

Thus, on average, nine credits will be returned for every 10 played.

This may not be an incredibly exciting machine, but at least there is a lot of little action. Since there are no big wins getting pulled out of the overall payout pool, the average player will split the $9 million pool in a more equitable manner than the other two machines, and each player will average a 90%

payback, or $90 returned on every $100 they bet.

The Small Potatoes payout structure features a lot of winners, albeit small ones.

COMPARING THE THREE MACHINES

The three machines we've shown—the Roll 'em Winner, the Mega-Machine, and the Small Potatoes—all share a 90% return. When all is said and done and everything holds perfectly to form, the players as an aggregate pool will win back $9 million of the $10 million they bet and the casino will win its 10%, which is $1 million.

Where these machines are not equal is in the manner in which the winning pool will be split. The machines on the two extremes—the Mega-Machine and Small Potatoes—are not realistic to today's market and wouldn't be successful or inviting to the players. On one extreme, you have the Mega-Machine, which provides the dream to one player, but essentially wipes out all other players. That is not enticing. On the other extreme, you have the Small Potatoes, which will make a lot of people mildly happy in a small way, but no one happy in a big way. That wouldn't work either as people play slots to hit jackpots.

The Mega-Machine and the Small Potatoes are not based on actual machines; they are only examples to illustrate how a payback schedule affects a player's chances of winning and, as discussed, neither would be successful slot machines.

The Roll 'em machine, on the other hand, is based on realistic paybacks, though the overall payback shown here would be loose based on penny machines and tight based on bigger denomination machines. The big incentive is still there in the Roll 'em, but at the same time, the little guys can grind away with small wins while waiting and hoping for the bigger one.

PROS AND CONS OF PLAYING THE WAPS

The extreme example above of the Mega-Machine illustrates, in an exaggerated fashion, the benefits and drawbacks of going for a monster progressive jackpot: You'll win less often by going for a monster progressive jackpot and overall you'll lose more. The big progressives will give you a decent overall return while you try for the big lucky break, thus keeping you marginally happy, perhaps enough to keep playing. But you won't win as often or as much as you might on the other machines available to you because of the amount of money put aside for the big jackpot.

In general, the larger the progressive type of jackpot the greater the percentage of money withheld. But if you're not the one hitting that jackpot, then you're the one paying for it.

I used the word "type" above when describing the progressives, because the return percentage on smaller wins for WAPs such as Quartermania and Megabucks is not adjusted as the jackpots grow, nor do they get better for the player when the jackpots are smaller. However, while a blanket statement can't cover all situations, you would expect that more modest progressives would provide the player with a better short-term return.

Let me summarize the advantages and disadvantages of playing WAPs. We'll look first at the reasons for not playing a WAP.

Reasons to Not Play a WAP

First, you're going to lose more money, on average, at these machines, often a lot more. Your bankroll will be drained much faster than a non-progressive machine. As far as I'm concerned, that's never a good strategy. You want your bankroll to hold firm and tight, and to get as much play out of your money as possible. You also want to give yourself the best chances of winning. Sometimes, you'll be putting in credits as fast as the casino can eat them without the casino being as reciprocal as you would like. That's a big downside to a WAP.

The second reason concerns the accumulation of points. You want to maximize your action at the machines so that you can earn the benefits afforded you by participation in the players clubs. I'm a big believer that hitting the "free buffet" spin, or "free or discounted room" spin, or "cash rebate" spin, or any of the other rewards given to slots players who show enough action, is well worth consideration as part of your winnings. The smaller the cost to get to comp-land, the better off you are. It's more enjoyable to talk about the fun when the steak and lobster is on the house.

Being able to get more action per dollar played should be a part of your winning strategy. Your $100 of action will go a lot longer with less of an edge against it. Wide area progressive will bleed your money much faster than standard slot machines.

Reasons to Play a WAP

Now, I'll explain the reason that you might want to play WAPs. The gravitational pull of multi-million dollar jackpots is too much to resist, even at the cost of some percentage points in return. For many, that's the whole point of playing the slot machines in the first place and the reason why wide area progressives are so popular.

With a lot of luck and the right timing, one spin can change your life. Whether it is the lottery or the big progressives, the attraction of one stroke in time changing everything is certainly something to think about.

WIDE AREA PROGRESSIVE SUMMARY

I've told you the good and bad about these big boys. It's your call now. I always like to go for the best odds, because that gives me the best chances of winning. And I like spending as little as I can to earn my comps. Personally, I'm not a dreamer when that dream is way out of my reach.

But it's your money and your dreams. If your goal is to try for that long shot, may the gods of luck be with you.

10 SECRETS OF LAS VEGAS LOCALS

Here are ten secrets of local Las Vegas slot players.

1. Slot machines can be addictive. The mesmerizing music and constant spinning of the reels can "hypnotize" you into playing longer, and for more money, that you intended to play.

2. Don't spend good money after bad. That is, accept a reasonable loss and go home when you've played the maximum amount of money you intended to play. Never put in more money trying to win back the money you've already lost.

3. Accept a small win and go home when the machines get cold and start gobbling up your win. Better to go home a small winner than any kind of loser.

4. If you have a history of being unable to stop playing even when you're losing, do not bring your ATM or credit cards with you to the casino. Bring only as much money with you as you intend to play that day.

5. Cashout vouchers are the same as cash. Treat them the same way.

6. When you cash out of a machine, immediately take your cashout voucher to a change machine. Converting vouchers into cash may prevent you from inserting more money into a machine than you would ordinarily play at one time.

7. Casinos that are off the Strip, commonly called "locals" casinos, pay out a higher percentage than Strip casinos.

8. Play on days when the casino is offering promotional bonuses to Players Card members. Typical bonuses include triple-points for your play, free play, half-points in casino restaurants. Most locals casinos also have one promotional day each week for seniors, when they offer people over the age of 55 triple points, free play, free seniors-only tournament entries, and even a free cup of Starbucks coffee.

9. Always swipe your players club card and punch in your pin number at a players club machine before you begin play. You must press the "accept offer" button on the menu to receive any bonuses you are eligible to receive that day.

10. Break a larger denomination bill into smaller denomination bills that are more in keeping with the amount of money you intend to play at any one time. Break a $100 bill into $20 bills if you usually play $20 at a time before you decide the machine is a loser and move along to a different machine.

21 WINNING STRATEGIES AT SLOTS

Players are always asking me, "How can there be winning strategies at slots? All you do is spin the reels and either win or lose, isn't that right?" The answer is no, that it isn't right. There are better ways to play and we'll go over them in this chapter.

There are ways to maximize your chances of winning in the short term by playing the proper amount of credits, strategies to increase your chances of hitting big jackpots, strategies to take advantage of the benefits casinos give to slots players, better casinos to play in and better machines to choose from, and finally, ways to maximize wins and minimize losses through money management strategies. Knowing how to properly play the slots can make the difference between winning and losing, and this chapter will show you those tips and secrets.

Surprisingly, there are lots of strategies you can pursue for such a simple game. By following my advice, you'll do much better than the average player and, at times and under the right conditions, you may actually find yourself with an edge. Let's get to it. Here is the first of my 21 winning strategy tips.

WINNING STRATEGY #1
Choose Better Casino Jurisdictions

Las Vegas casinos, on average, give small and medium coin players ($1 and less) a much better shake at the machines than their Atlantic City counterparts. Large credit players ($5 and up) have a similar game in either jurisdiction, based on the last figures I've seen. I examined reports published by both the Nevada State Gaming Control Board and the New Jersey Casino Control Commission and saw significant differences in payback percentages.

So, for this winning slots tip, if you are a small or medium coin player and have a choice, play Las Vegas slots over Atlantic City slots. In fact, you will want to choose Las Vegas over many other places. But of course, that is not always practical. But this is not just about playing Las Vegas; it is also advice on where to play in Las Vegas. In other words, if you are a serious player looking for the best odds, which means, your best chances of winning, are you better off heading away from the tourism centers to more local casinos.

How about the rest of you slots players taking on the slots in the riverboat states, Indian reservations, and various other locations that contain slot machines? The general rule is that the more competition in an area, the better the odds.

Since you generally have little choice in choosing areas to play—basically where you happen to be is where you'll play—use the other winning tips presented in this chapter for maximizing your odds at the slots. When you are playing slots in Louisiana or Illinois, it does you no good to know that the odds may be better in Las Vegas—just as it does a New Yorker no good to know that bagels are better in Brooklyn when he happens to be in California, or that movies might be $2 less in San Francisco when he is currently at home in Manhattan.

However, if you're in a competitive environment like Las Vegas, there are plenty of choices on where to play. Below is a chart showing the average payout percentages by credit amount in Nevada casinos, as published by the Nevada Gaming Control Board, for the one-year period beginning July

1, 2014 and ending June 30, 2015. All electronic machines including slots, video poker and video keno are included in these numbers.

LAS VEGAS SLOTS PERCENTAGES

PAYBACK PERCENTAGE BY CREDIT
Las Vegas Area Slot Percentages

1¢ Slot Machines
The Strip—88.24%
Downtown—88.72%
Boulder Strip—90.24%
N. Las Vegas—90.56%

5¢ Slot Machines
The Strip—92.00%
Downtown—92.34%
Boulder Strip—95.58%
N. Las Vegas—95.43%

25¢ Slot Machines
The Strip—91.21%
Downtown—94.67%
Boulder Strip—96.59%
N. Las Vegas—96.48%

$1 Slot Machines
The Strip—93.69%
Downtown—95.24%
Boulder Strip—95.66%
N. Las Vegas—96.12%

You can see that the larger the denomination of credits played on the Las Vegas Strip, the greater the average payback percentage given by the casino. This is no coincidence. Casinos would like to encourage players to play at the higher credit levels and encourage them to do so by paying out more for the larger credits. While this is not posted anywhere in the casino, nor is it common knowledge, players know when they're having success at a machine and when they're not. Higher percentage payouts do get noticed, and with player-win satisfaction at a reasonable level, the credits keep flowing and players keep playing.

But notice what happens when you get off the Strip where income from slot machines are less important to casinos' overall bottom line and go to downtown Las Vegas, and particularly the outskirts of the city, places like Boulder Strip and North Las Vegas. The return to the player goes up. For example a penny machine returns on average 88.24% on the Strip (that's an 11.76% disadvantage) but over 2% higher on the Boulder corridor and North Las Vegas. That 2% difference might not sound like a lot but it is actually a significant number when you multiply it by every single spin of the machine.

The numbers are particularly striking on the 25¢ machines, which are a full 5% better on the outskirts of Las Vegas.

The idea of paying higher percentages to big-denomination players mirrors the thinking as to the placement of machines. More frequent winners means players stay encouraged to play the higher levels and the machines get more action. Translation: more profits. While casinos make less percentage-wise from the higher credit machines, they more than make up for it in action and overall profits.

ATLANTIC CITY SLOTS PERCENTAGES

In Atlantic City, the payback percentages for lower denomination machines ($1 or less) are significantly lower than in the more competitive Las Vegas casino environment, with average paybacks 3%-6% less. On the $5, $25, and larger machines, the paybacks are competitive with Las Vegas big-credit machines. In Atlantic City, you'll never play a machine that pays out less than 83%. The New Jersey Casino Control Commission requires that slot machines in Atlantic City pay back at least that amount on all slot machines.

INDIAN CASINO SLOTS PERCENTAGES

It would be impossible to generalize slot percentages at the Indian casinos in the United States because there are hundreds of tribal casinos ranging from giant ones like Mohegan Sun and Foxwoods to tiny ones tucked away in less populous areas. But the general rules will apply. When there is competition, machines will tend to return more money to the players and you also will have the opportunity to shop around and choose the casino that best serves your slots action.

RIVERBOATS AND OTHER JURISDICTIONS

Until Atlantic City began offering gambling in 1978, Las Vegas was the only U.S. state with legalized gambling. Now as we are well into the 2000s, almost every U.S. state has legalized gambling or has Indian tribes operating casinos. Casinos have proliferated in Canada as well. As with the Indian casino, no blanket statement can be made covering slots percentages, but go with the general guidelines discussed above—the more competition, the better for you. To find out more about slots percentages in your area, you can go on the Internet and search under your state gaming commission. They often publish the slots hold percentages, so you can get better educated on the average payback by denominations in your state.

CONCLUSION

The lesson here: Competition is good for you. Play in casino jurisdictions where competing casinos are vying against each other for your business. As to individual casinos, this second point is our next winning strategy.

WINNING STRATEGY #2
Play at Casinos That Cater to Slots Players

Your first rule as a player is to go where the machines give you the best chances of winning. That means you want to concentrate your play at casinos where slots players are a primary source of income. If a casino is looking to attract slots players, it will give you something to whoop about so that it can keep you as a steady player. This means having machines with a good payback. Players figure out quickly how long their money lasts, especially the players that take their weekly check down to the casinos. If your money gets drained time and again with little play to show for it, you will tire of the failure and go elsewhere where better success promises more positive reinforcement.

It's a simple fact. Better paying machines draw more players. Many casinos nowadays ignore this principle and their total slots handle suffers for this.

How do you get a sense of when a casino is good for slots players? If the casino is buzzing with slots players, that's a good sign. It's not the end in itself, but it is a sign that slots players are enjoying themselves. It's similar to scoping out a restaurant in an unfamiliar area. Lots of patrons is a good sign. An empty casino doesn't bode well. Go where the action is.

WINNING STRATEGY #3
Avoid Sucker Joints

I've already talked about looking for places that have lots of players, so obviously the converse is true: Avoid places where there are few players. Few players typically means "few winning players." Lack of competition or the proverbial "only place in town" often translates to poor odds, or as I like to call them—sucker machines.

But there's another principle that is very true as well: Do not play slots in places where the slots business is incidental to the main business. Why? Because the customers that play the machines in these establishments are not there to play the machines. They are there to do something else. They see the machines, impulsively dump some credits into them, and then move on. These types of slots venues can get away with horrific odds because the players aren't there to play the slots. They are passing through on the way to somewhere else.

The thinking here is that the player will drop credits into the machines gratuitously. And that in fact is what happens at these venues.

In Nevada, where gambling is permitted seemingly everywhere, if you want to get good odds, avoid playing slot machines in the following places: airports, laundromats, bars, grocery and convenience stores, supermarkets, gas stations, and the like. These are places where slot machines will swallow your money as fast as you can feed them.

WINNING STRATEGY #4
Avoid Sucker Machines

In terms of finding machines that give you better percentages, locations within a casino are often important as well. That slot machine in the bathroom can be counted on to have the worst payback in the entire casino. Think about it: Who is going to be hanging around a bathroom very long for the purpose of gambling? Slots lining a restaurant or buffet line are generally set with lower percentages since the average player will have just seconds or minutes of playing time before his or her spot moves closer to the gluttony that awaits in the dining area. This is not an area for a serious slots player. These machines are just there to catch loose change.

Serious players are going to park themselves in front of machines for hours on end, but will only do so if they get enough positive reinforcement. Winning spins is their currency. Stick serious players in front of enough lemons, and that casino won't be seeing them again.

WINNING STRATEGY #5
Always Use a Player Card

Make sure you join the slots club in every casino you patronize. Your first order of business in any casino you enter is to head to the slots club desk and sign up for the players club. If you are already a member but have forgotten or lost your card, get your replacement card. You just need to show your ID and the casino will be glad to make another one for you. There is no charge for new or lost cards. Membership is free. The casino is happy to have you as a slots customer and will do everything it can to keep you as a player.

Now the important part: Make sure to always insert your players club card into the slot machine before you start playing. You accrue points every time you spin the reels and they add up to a wealth of benefits. You are costing yourself money by not inserting your card into the machine.

Points equal money. Make sure you get yours.

WINNING STRATEGY #6
Playing the Proper Credit

Depending upon the machine, you have a choice of playing anywhere from one to five credits at a time on a typical classic slot machine, and penny video slots allow you to play one hundred credits at a time and sometimes as many as five hundred or one thousand credits!

A very important principle to keep in mind at classic slot machines that pay proportionately more for all credits played is to play the maximum number of credits allowed on each play so that you can maximize your gain if you hit the jackpot. For example, one credit might pay 800, two credits 1,600, and three credits 4,000. That's a big difference. If you're uncomfortable playing at that denomination because playing the full number of credits is over your budget, you may be able to find smaller denomination machines that allow your bankroll to handle the full credit allowance. Obviously, on a machine with a disproportionate payoff for more credits, you want to take advantage of it.

However, on the penny slots it is a different consideration. For one, playing the maximum amount the game allows on penny video slots simply means that you will receive a proportionately larger payout on winning lines—hitting the best combination does not mean forfeiting credits you would have lost because max coins weren't played. There are some penny video slots that do require max coins played to hit a designated jackpot, but these machines are the exception rather than the rule. In any case, check out the payout schedules so that you are aware of which type of machine you are playing.

There is a secondary factor about playing max coins on a penny machine and it is a really important one—money management. If you are viewing the penny slots as anything resembling a penny slot—in other words, you really are playing for pennies—then what are you doing playing max coins when it can cost you several dollars a play! That would be crazy.

If you're playing buy-your-pay classic machines, you absolutely must play the full number of credits to get the benefits of not only the big jackpot payout, but also the lesser ones, which may be void if you didn't put enough credits in.

WINNING STRATEGY #7
Make Smart Bankroll Decisions

As a player, you have a choice of a large variety of machines, from the 1¢ slots, 5¢, 10¢, 25¢, 50¢, $1.00, $5.00, $25.00 and even higher credit machines. While the larger denomination slots tend to average a higher rate of return, moving up in coin value to get a better percentage should not be a factor in choosing a machine if it causes you to make larger bets than you can handle. That is a formula for disaster and nothing good will come of it.

The most important factor before ever approaching any machine, gaming table, or any type of gamble, is to determine the amount you're willing to gamble. You should never, under any circumstances, gamble with money you cannot afford to lose either financially or emotionally. That is a rule that can never be broken if you are going to be a smart gambler. So before you ask yourself the question, "What is the best denomination machine to play?" first ask yourself how much you are willing to put up, as your playing stake will determine the proper type of machine you should play. And be sure to read the money management chapter carefully where I talk about this issue in-depth.

Though it is true that, as an industry average, the higher the denomination credit played the greater the winning percentage returned by the casinos, do not get waylaid by this information. As I've stated earlier, every machine has its own dynamic. An IGT 25¢ Double Diamond machine may pay 91% while the exact type of 25¢ Double Diamond next to it on the bank may give out 96%. A 5¢ machine across the way may pay back 97%, while the one next to it may give back only 88%. Each machine must be viewed on a case-by-case basis so that the best and most optimal strategy might be followed.

While the general winning formula follows the guideline of playing the games and making the bets that afford you the best odds, there is one overriding factor that comes first for winning players—money management.

The first playing decision is to decide the proper amount you're willing to wager. Never play at a level of risk or affordability that is over your head, and that goes for all stages of gambling. Play the games and stakes that are at your level and you will never suffer a terrible loss.

At the slot machines, you don't want to bet over your head, especially not for an extra percent or two. Face it: It's much better to play x amount at a 95% payback (5% house edge) than four times x amount at a 96% payback (4% edge). While you might lose less percentage-wise at the larger bet, you can lose almost four times as much money overall because of the higher stakes being played. That never makes sense when the lower and more comfortable stakes are the right fit for you.

Don't lose sight of your overall goal in playing slots—to relax and have a good time. That can only be done while playing within your means and at stakes you're comfortable with. If the best percentage you can get at a slot machine that you want to play is 93%, that's fine. If you can grab 95% or even 99%, so much the better. Keep to these basics—having fun—and you can't go wrong. Think about all that while eating your comped buffet and watching the comped show.

WINNING STRATEGY #8
Bump Up to Single Credit Play

Here's an inside tip for improving your odds at the machines. I spoke earlier about playing the maximum number of credits to get the best odds, and how larger denomination machines average a higher payback percentage. Sometimes you'll find classic machines you like at a one-step higher denomination that don't penalize you for playing less than the full number of credits. For example, you may find a machine that gives you the same proportionately for the first credit played as the third or fifth credit, or whatever number of credits.

All things being equal, if you like the same machine at a higher denomination than you usually play—bump up! For example, if you're a quarter player (investing three or five quarters per pull, 75¢ or $1.25), bump up to the $1 machine at single credit play. Similarly, a 5¢ player can move up to the 25¢ machines, and a $1 player can bump up to the $5 machines. You are not increasing the cost of your plays as I warned in Winning Strategy #7 above, you are only increasing the percentage payback.

This is a great way to take advantage of the higher percentages being paid on the larger denomination machines. Remember, this strategy is only good when there is no penalty for single-credit play. One other caution that is very, very important: Never double-bump denominations. That is, don't go from 5¢ to $1, or 25¢ to $5 machines. Money management is of utmost importance in the winning formula, and betting over your bankroll, which a double bump will do, would be a terrible decision.

The single bump with a single credit play is the maximum correct play.

WINNING STRATEGY #9
Get Away from Cold Machines

You'll sometimes find a machine that is so cold that you can't seem to win anything. This machine may be set so tight that you're feeling the pain. You need love, not pain. If a slot machine is not paying for you, you need to change machines and get one that will put a smile on your face.

Besides the lack of success, there is another reason to leave: You're most likely not enjoying yourself. In the back of your mind, you're thinking that you should leave the machine and try another. Follow your instincts. Don't put more credits into a machine that feels bad.

Cardinal rule: If you're not comfortable with a particular machine, go to one where you are comfortable. After all, why play machines that give you bad feelings? Stick to the slots that give you a positive feeling, as that's where you'll get your maximum enjoyment.

If it ain't paying, you shouldn't be playing.

WINNING STRATEGY #10
Don't Leave a Hot Machine

When a machine is hot and paying off for you like crazy, play if for all it's worth. A hot machine generally means you have found a machine with a high payback return, a loose one. Don't leave that machine! It wouldn't take but a few seconds from the time you got up from your seat before another savvy player zoomed in on that nest egg like a mother hen, clucking away as the payouts continued.

However, should the tide start to turn and money starts being sucked back into the machine, use smart money management principles and leave the machine with winnings in your ledger. That's always a smart way to play.

Similarly, if your machine is paying so-so, and you see another player leave a machine that's been hot, grab that machine while it's still available. You always want to play the machine that appears to be the best payer because it usually is the best payer.

STICK WITH A WINNING MACHINE

Let me repeat this: Unless you have really had enough play for a day or need to go elsewhere, don't ever leave a winning machine. When you have a hot one, ride it for all it's worth. But once it stops paying well, back off, and then take a break—with all your profits.

IMPORTANT POINT
Understanding Hot and Cold Advice

Don't take my advice on playing hot machines and avoiding cold ones to mean that I think slot machine spins are on a memory basis concerning winners and losers—because they're not.

Machines are not "due" for anything, not for a win, not for a loss, not for spinning over and doing cartwheels. Each spin of the reel is independently generated and has as much to do with the next spin as it did with the last spin—that is, nothing. They're random, or are at least as close to being random as the manufacturers can make them, which is very close to truly random. There are probabilities of reels lining up in a certain way and the payout for winners is paid on those probabilities.

When I talk about hot and cold machines, I only speak of using the recent history of the machines to understand that there may be a pattern of better or worse payouts, a pattern that is tied in to the probabilities of how the machine was set. While a small sampling is really not sufficient for a true empirical determination, barring anything else to the contrary, it's all the information you have.

WINNING STRATEGY #11
Wide-Area Progressives (WAP) Strategy

Wide-area progressives (WAP) are progressive slot machines linked together across many casinos such that the jackpots rise to high levels. The odds of winning one of these jackpots is one in maybe 50 million and, accordingly, the jackpot can grow as high as several hundred million dollars. They pay back less than 90%, which means their edge over you is a pretty big 10%+, and that includes the returns for the jackpot winner. When you take out that one lucky winner, the drain is much worse. The other issue is that it is so difficult to hit the WAP—on average, they are only hit once a year, more or less—so I think, why bother? Of course, if you do hit it, you'll be incredibly happy but that's such a longshot of longshots that it's not really worth thinking about—not when I believe there are better plays out there for you.

You go for a wide-area progressive jackpot only if you don't mind a high loss rate while you're chasing. I suggest the lotto instead if you're going for a big play or, if you like progressives, a local area progressive (LAP) which spreads the wealth around a lot better.

Let's look at the LAP machines next.

WINNING STRATEGY #12
Local-Area Progressives (LAP) Strategy

A local area progressive (LAP), also called a proprietary progressive, are progressive slot machines linked together within a casino and typically owned and operated by that casino. There could be a half dozen or a dozen machines linked together to many dozens, depending upon the size of the casino. The more machines linked together, the faster the progressive jackpot tends to rise.

Playing local area progressives is a much better percentage play than playing the larger progressives. Since less money is being taken out to feed the big progressive jackpot compared to the WAP, there is more money to spread around to the players and you'll get more play out of the machines. That is, you'll last longer and have a better chance of walking away with money even if you don't hit the big one.

Also, while the prize is not nearly as big as a WAP, you have a shot at winning a jackpot, since these are hit on a fairly frequent basis.

The LAP is a play I like a lot better than getting drained by a big linked WAP jackpot.

WINNING STRATEGY #13
Standalone Progressive (SAP) Strategy

The third type of progressive machine is called a standalone progressive. A standalone progressive (SAP) machine is an island to itself and is not linked to any other machine. The progressive jackpot rises every time a credit is played in the machine until a jackpot is hit by a lucky player, at which time the jackpot gets reset to the minimum amount. The standalone progressives feature the smallest jackpots of the three types of progressives, because only one machine generates the rising progressive as opposed to the LAP and especially the WAP, which link multiple machines.

When you're in a casino that has a variety of standalone progressives, shop around for the highest jackpot. There will be a wide disparity between the smallest jackpot, which will be the machine most recently hit, and the biggest jackpot, which of course, is the machine whose jackpot has been dormant the longest.

It almost goes without saying—but you'll always see clueless players giving action to inferior machines—to always play the machines with the highest jackpot. I don't know how many times I've seen shortsighted players dropping credits into a progressive machine when a similar machine several banks away, or even one bank away, contained a much higher jackpot. Why settle for a smaller jackpot while still having the same risk? Of course, a wide-area progressive will have the same progressive total on every machine since they are all linked together, but the standalone progressive machines will vary.

Again, with all things being equal, always play for the bigger jackpot. This is a very important winning tip for progressive players.

WINNING STRATEGY #14
Play Max Credits on Progressives

The principle of playing max coins to hit the big prize holds true on all progressives. On progressive slots, the full number of credits must be played to win the big jackpot. Any lesser number of credits will negate the big jackpot and give you only a minor win at the machine, that is, minor compared to the riches you could have had.

You sometimes see players putting in minimum credits at a progressive to preserve their bankroll. It's one of the worst moves you can make in a casino because not only can't you succeed in the goal of winning the jackpot—which is why you're playing the progressive in the first place—but you're enduring horrible odds along the way.

I saw a progressive machine some years back where the difference between hitting the big prize playing with two credits, which was 25,000 credits on the quarter machine ($6,250) and the three credits payout (max credits) was enormous, enough to make the player sick had he played one or two coins as opposed to the full three coins. How much was the full credit payout? $615,000!

If you're going to go for it, go for it. Max credits all the time.

WINNING STRATEGY #15
Tournament Slots Strategy

One way to maximize your return at the machines is through slot tournaments. While a full discussion of tournaments is beyond the scope of this book, a few items are worth noting. If you are a tournament player, you'll want to pick the tournaments that give you the best return for the dollar invested, not only in terms of prize money but in the comps the casino is willing to give you as part of the tournament package.

By picking and choosing between tournaments, you can find attractive packages that can perfectly fit your needs. Sometimes, when you add up all the benefits to the prize money offered, you find yourself with a really sweet deal. As a member of a slots club, the casinos will keep you well informed of their tournament schedules. You can also get on the list of other casinos, or check the gambling magazines for ads advertising upcoming tournaments. The best way to find out about tournaments, however, is to get on the mailing lists.

The strategy in tournaments is very simple: hit the buttons as fast as you can. If your playing hand must get used for something else, like a bad itch, for example, get the other hand banging the buttons so you don't miss a beat.

Slot tournaments are very popular among players and if you are a good player you may find yourself comped to some of them!

WINNING STRATEGY #16
Finding the Loosest/Tightest Slots in a Casino

The placement of loose and tight slot machines and the actual paybacks of a casino's slot machines, are about the closest kept secrets in a casino. Neither the slots manager, slots hosts, nor slots attendants know the percentages of any of the machines or where the best ones are located. The one or two management personnel who know what is what keep tight-lipped about the whole thing and to nary a soul do they whisper these secrets.

Machines are not placed haphazardly. Slot machine placement is a carefully thought-out science. The profits from the slot machines account for most of a typical casino's income, and it is up to the operators to decide how to maximize those profits. They plan where to best position their loosest slot machines, where the medium payers should go, and where the tight machines, the ones that hold the highest house edge, are best positioned. Generating strategies for maximizing profits in a casino is a science where operators look at everything—from the best places to locate gaming tables and slots machines right down to the scents that are put in the air.

Ignore what you might read otherwise in other books or hear from uninformed players. Slot machine placement is a carefully strategized art with a goal of maximizing profits. If you can get into a casino's mindset, and think along with the casino, it will open up clues on hot and cold machine placement.

Casinos take their slots profits seriously, as well they should. Look at how much Vegas has grown; it's hardly the product of haphazard planning. The first thing you need to understand is the strategy behind slot machine placement. The cardinal rule in attracting slots players to the machines is to get them excited. Bang, bang, clank, clank. If credits are mounting and bells and whistles are trumpeting from winning machines, you can be sure that adrenaline is flowing through the veins of the players in the slots area.

Casinos want to place the loose machines in visible areas where players are in a position to stay and play, as opposed to drop and run. Thus, central areas within a slots pit, like a corner machine visible from several aisles where the slots players are, may be a good spot for a loose machine. The loose machines will be sprinkled throughout strategic areas, so the excitement of frequent winners can spread throughout the slots area and keep interest high.

On the other hand, aisle machines facing out from the slots area, while visible, tend to attract drop-and-run players, thus; they are generally set tighter. Passers-by are going elsewhere and while they may drop some credits into the machines, they have a different destination on their mind. Slot machines facing open aisles also tend to be tighter for the simple reason that regular players do not like to sit with their back to busy aisles. It's an uncomfortable setting for a slots player. The heart of a slots area is a more comfortable place to relax and play for hours. Regulars are surrounded by their own kind.

The worst machines are generally found along the buffet and restaurant lines, waiting areas for the show, and other like areas. Players who tend to drop credits in these machines often do so to kill time.

If you're a frequent player to a slots area, you'll begin to notice which machines seem to pay better. If they seem to be better machines, that is, looser, they most probably are. The best way to determine machines that seem to be kicking up the most action, however, is by asking the cocktail waitresses and slots attendants who work the area, day after day, night after night. They notice the better machines and they know the stinkers. Ask them nicely, and you may get a great tip that will put you close to a 99% paybacker.

Does this give you definitive information on which machines in particular are actually the best to play? No, but it does give you information to work with. You know to avoid the machines in the areas we've identified as most likely to contain tight machines. That's a start. And while you know that loose machines aren't identified in the casinos, the more frequent winnings associated with certain machines will become obvious over time by either your own careful observation, or that of regular players or casino slot employees you could ask. And once you get that figured out, your chances of winning become greatly improved.

WINNING STRATEGY #17
Getting an Actual Advantage at the Machines

If you play things right, you may at times have the actual advantage, or close to it, if the full effective value of the comps are added in to the house edge. That's right, when all is said and done, you can at times find a situation that actually gives you the edge at slots! Amazing, but true.

Let's say your slots club has an aggressive incentive program and they run a big promotion with all sorts of goodies, cash rebates, and loose machines. You show up at the casino, grab the comp or discounted room, sit down to a free buffet with your companion, and after three trips to the food line and one to the dessert bar (or about three trips too many) you head to the machines.

The casino has spiced the floor with some 99+% payback slot machines, and using my techniques, you discover one and settle in for some serious play. You enter your card into the machine and start racking up playing time. The machine is hot, but you keep cool with the drinks. A friendly cocktail waitress takes interest in your play and seems to come by frequently. That's good, the drinks are refreshing and they're flowing.

Credits are racking up and bells are going off. You're really having a good time, so much so that after your companion says it's time for the comped show, you realize that those two hours that went by fast were really four and half, a mini-marathon session at the slots.

A great show with two complimentary drinks, a few more hours at the machines, this time with some losses, but adding the end result to the afternoon session, you're still a few hundred ahead. You've done better than your expected 1% loss, a good day indeed, but you have really scored on the incentive program. You've racked up the action for the casino, earned a full 1% cash rebate, plus piled on the comps—tee shirts, deck of cards and dice, more free meals and rooms, another show—and more. Not a bad day at all. When you add that all up, you've even enjoyed the edge when all the benefits are given their full value.

Now, things won't always be quite this rosy but if you stick to loose machines, avoid obvious stinkers, and practice smart money management principles, you've given the casino a good game and have done just what you love to do—play the slots. At the same time, you've reaped all the benefits of the players club and planted seeds for your next trip.

Win or lose, the casino is happy with your play. The buffet lines might cost them a few dollars, and the room may be a third the stated price when the overhead is taken into account. But they'll have a happy player who enjoyed the stay and the play, and most likely will come back again.

And for you, the recipient of these comps, you're getting the full value of everything you can get.

WINNING STRATEGY #18
Avoid Neighbors of Hot Machines

Casinos place tight slot machines next to loose machines, and mix average machines into the plan so that they can extract the maximum profits from their slots placement. The loose machines serve the purpose of generating excitement and action, the tight machines try to extract a larger winning percentage, and the average machines do some of both.

There is no reason for a casino to place one loose machine next to another one. In fact, it would be poor placement. One loose machine is all it takes to generate excitement for that little area. So you would rarely find loose machines set side by side. There is even another reason. Knowing that players play side-by-side with their friends, they are able to get away with a lemon as they capitalize on the fact that people who travel together play together. The lesser percentage that casinos make on the loose machines comes right back by tightening up on the two machines next to it. One hand feeds the other, so to speak.

You take advantage of this knowledge by avoiding machines placed next to hot machines. When you see a machine paying off like crazy and, unfortunately, you're not the one for whom those bells are tolling, avoid those adjacent machines. They'll be dry like the desert air.

If you're a serious player looking to get the best odds possible at the slots and you're with a playing companion, you need to split up so that one can handle the loose machine and the other one can find the next one. To maximize your winning chances, you just can't sit next to one another.

WINNING STRATEGY #19
Play One Machine Only

You'll often see fanatical slots players working two machines at a time. Really ambitious players may play three slots simultaneously. Now that's action! The advantage of playing multiple machines is that you get more action, and by getting more action and having two machines working for you, you will hit winners more frequently.

However, there is a disadvantage to playing multiple machines—this advice is really a corollary of the advice in Winning Strategy #18—beyond putting more money at risk. If it is poor strategy to play two machines together, obviously, you should play one machine by itself, avoiding the tempting machines on either side. You cannot afford to lose the extra percentage points you gain from finding and playing a hot-paying machine by handing those winning credits right back to the tight machine situated next to it.

That is not a good approach. Play only one machine at a time!

WINNING STRATEGY #20
Playing Non-Progressive Slots After a Jackpot

Many players think that a regular non-progressive machine that has just been hit for a big winner is no longer "due" and should be avoided like the plague. This is a fallacy. Slot machines have no memory of wins and losses and are set to completely random standards. Every spin is independent of the spin before it. It is like a pair of dice. They don't remember that a 7 was just rolled, and thus the chances of another 7 being rolled is the same as it always was and always will be—one chance in six.

While slot machines are certainly more "intelligent" than a pair of dice, the processing power of their computer chips is used only to allow random spins for each time the reels are set in motion. There is no preset order of winning combinations or trigger that sets in motion a different set of possibilities based on whether the last spin was a winner or a loser. It is random and has a fresh start every time the reels are spun.

Therefore, if a machine hits the jackpot on spin one, that doesn't lessen the chances one iota that it won't hit that same jackpot combination on spin two. At the same time, it doesn't increase the odds either, but the point is this: You've got a hot machine that is spewing out winners. That's what you look for in a casino.

Of course, if you're been gambling for a while, hitting a jackpot is a perfect time to take a break. But if you're still geared for action, don't abandon the horse that just won you the race!

WINNING STRATEGY #21
Playing Progressive Slots After a Jackpot

In the above example, we talked about hitting the big payout on a machine that was hot, and sticking with that machine if you were still in the gambling mood. But that was for non-progressive machines. Everything changes when the discussion turns to a progressive machine. Once a progressive jackpot is hit, whether that jackpot is linked to other machines in the casino throughout a larger jurisdiction, or even resides solely on the machine itself, the smart move is to immediately call it quits with the machine you're playing and with any other machine that is linked to that progressive system.

Because when the jackpot hits on a progressive, the machine gets reset to the starting amount, which is the bare minimum. You want a ripe, juicy fruit to go after, not the pit.

Your average percentage payback in slots, what is referred to as "loose" or "tight," is dependent on the payback chart listed on the machine itself. In a progressive, a jackpot that has swelled because it hasn't been hit in a while would be a loose machine. If it has swelled enough, it could even be a profitable machine. A dry progressive, one that has been recently hit, would be a tight one.

To illustrate the principle, I'll use an example of 100 balls, sixty of them red, thirty-nine of them green, and one of them blue. If you pick a ball blindly from the mix and it is green, you win $1; if it is blue, $20; and if it is red, you lose $1. Every time you finish picking, you throw the ball back in the mix and try again. This analogy is pretty close to what actually occurs with slot machine payouts, only in this simple example, there are only two winning combinations, the green and blue, not ten or twenty as you might find at an actual machine.

Let's examine what the chances of winning are. Thirty-nine green balls will pay you $1 each for a total of $39. One blue ball will pay you $20. You have a total of $59 you can win against $60 you could lose. Overall, out of every hundred balls picked at $1 each, the expectation would be a $1 loss. That translates to a 1% house edge, a very loose machine.

Let's now presume that this is a progressive game and, since the blue balls haven't been picked in a while, it has risen to the high value of a $20 payout from its original starting payout of $10—the example we used earlier. On your next pick, bingo, you get the blue ball and get paid $20 for your good luck.

Great, let's say you're up $15 in the game now, but since the blue ball, the "progressive" was hit, the winning combination is now reset to $10, the starting point. This changes everything. Let's examine what your payback percentage would be with this new set of circumstances. Your odds of winning are still exactly the same as before, but your payouts for these wins are not! Thirty-nine greens pays you $39 as before, sixty reds loses you $60, also as before, but the blue now pays only $10. The winning combinations total $49 and the losing combinations total $60, for an expected net loss on every hundred picks of $11, or an 11% house edge. This is not a loose slot at all. Whereas you had a great game going before, giving you just a 1% nut to crack, you're now way behind the curve at this progressive game.

This illustrates the difference between your chance of hitting a winner, what is called your hit frequency, or frequency of winning, as opposed to your payback percentage—quite different concepts. Your frequency of winning didn't change after the blue ball was picked. There were still forty ways to win (thirty-nine greens and one blue), and sixty ways to lose (the sixty reds). Your frequency of winning here is 40%, which is much higher than you would find at an average machine, especially a progressive.

The payback percentage, as I showed above, has taken a drastic discount, because your jackpot (which has a frequency of occurrence of one in a hundred, or 1%) is worth only $10 now, not $20 as before. Your game went from being very good to being very poor.

Going back to real life slots, this is the exact principle that applies to your machines. Your frequency of winning doesn't change just because the jackpot was hit nor, for that matter, does your chances of hitting that jackpot on the next spin. But the problem is that your percentage payback has dropped like a stone over the abyss and you're getting terrible odds.

The conclusion: You want to stay away from progressives that have just been hit and, conversely, play ones that are hanging like ripe fruit with big payouts waiting for the lucky winner.

JACKPOTS & TAXES

Before I begin this chapter, let me alert you to the fact that I am neither an accountant, a lawyer, nor an expert on tax law. If indeed you do manage to win a large jackpot, you will be best served by hiring competent help to determine the proper reporting of gambling income and deductions to the IRS or other tax body that may apply. In other words, while on your jackpot vacation, don't use my advice as your final source; peel off a bill or two and give it to the pros.

Just the same, I'll provide some very general guidelines below.

Casinos are required by law to ensure that any single slot machine payout of $1,200 or over is reported to the Internal Revenue Service. A W-2G tax form must immediately be completed by the $1,200 winner at the casino. This form will be quickly forwarded to the IRS.

The W-2G form is comparable to the W-2 form you receive from your employer. The W-2 verifies the amount of money you have made in any given period of time, while the W-2G validates the money you received in slot machine winnings. The total dollar amount on the W-2G is added to your earnings on your W-2 form to determine your total taxable income for the year. For example, if your annual household income is $30,000 and you won $2,000 playing the slots, your total taxable income for the year would increase to $32,000.

Two valid forms of identification must be made available to the casino at the time of any big win. These might include a driver's license, credit card, or social security card.

The U.S. government allows slot machine gamblers to deduct losses up to, but not exceeding, the amount won. If you won a $2,000 jackpot in one year playing the slots, but lost a miscellaneous total of $2,500 in that same year, you would not be able to take the $500 difference as a loss off of your taxes.

The losses to be offset against winnings can't be subtracted directly from the itemized winnings; they must be taken separately as a miscellaneous deduction. This way the government is able to see exact winnings and exact losses. Losses from the previous year will not be accepted as losses for the present year. If that $2,500 loss had come from the previous year's play, you would be unable to deduct it against the current year's $2,000 win.

If you win a jackpot under $1,200, the casino is not required to report your winnings.

KEEPING LOGBOOKS

If you're a serious player, it is important to keep itemized logs of daily amounts won and lost at the slot machines—so that if you do win a jackpot, you can offset the jackpot total against all the losses it took to get you there. Dates, times and places are important to include in these journals. Keeping the names of any employees or witnesses who are able to verify your losses might be helpful. All of this may seem tedious, but when forced to deal with the Internal Revenue Service, your records can never be too detailed.

A simple way to tally daily wins and losses is to carry a small notebook, diary or journal. This will make it easy for you to jot down information as you play. If someone is playing with you, both of you may want to take turns recording necessary information. All transactions should be accounted for after each gambling session. The more verification you have of loss deductions, the more substantial and acceptable your loss claims will be.

Even if you're only playing casually, it may be wise to keep at least an informal record, as you never know when you might hit the jackpot. It will also let you know, in black and white, how you have done at the machines.

Sometimes the IRS demands additional evidence for gambling losses. These might include airline tickets, hotel bills, gas receipts or signed documents from witnesses who are able to verify your losses. Witnesses could be other players, slots attendants, slots hosts, or a casino supervisor. If you do hit the jackpot, the time put into this documentation will be well worth the trouble.

Players club members may also get loss documentation from the casinos. Their sophisticated tracking systems keep tally of everything—hours played, amount of credits bet, wins and losses, credit denominations—all for the purpose of tracking your action and giving you comps for your good play. If you nail a jackpot or two, this documentation is indisputable evidence for your claim. Again, you will need to seek competent tax advice from a professional should you hit some big wins, and especially if you hit a monster jackpot.

MONEY MANAGEMENT & WINNING

Managing your money is the first step toward being a winning player. Piling up several hundred dollars on a hot streak means nothing if you immediately turn around and lose it all—and then some.

A player that consistently gives his winnings back to the casino is a player that doesn't give himself a chance to win—in a sense, a player who refuses to win. No matter how well a session is going, this player feels the need to keep playing until his or her money is gone. Only an unusually long winning streak or a monster jackpot can put this player into the win column. It's as if the goal is to lose—and if he can't lose it today, there's always tomorrow.

For players hell-bent on losing, it doesn't take long for the odds to cooperate.

Losing is not what this book is about. I'm trying to teach you how to win. Part of this formula involves the use of the winning techniques and strategies described throughout this book. Another part, the most important part, is money management. If you don't handle your money with an intelligent plan from the start, you're going to come out a loser just about every time.

Here are the five principles of money management.

5 MONEY MANAGEMENT PRINCIPLES

1. The Winning Attitude

First and foremost is having a winning attitude. To be a winner, you have to genuinely want to be a winner.

2. Play Within Your Means

You must play within your means. We'll discuss bankroll considerations and optimal bet size for your bankroll in a moment. We'll also discuss loss limits.

3. Protect Your Winning Streaks

You need to protect your winning streaks. We'll talk a lot about restricting losses; this section shows you how to guard the winnings. There are some basic principles that must always be followed.

4. Emotional Control

You must have emotional control. You have to be able to handle your money and not let yourself be overwhelmed by the gambling atmosphere.

5. Stick to Your Original Limits

Money management is all about sticking to the original limits you decided on before sitting down at the machines. You can never allow yourself to take such a beating at the slots that you not only ruin your vacation but also lose more money than you can afford to lose.

Let's look at each of these money management elements in turn.

1. THE WINNING ATTITUDE

I see blackjack and craps players, poker players, video poker and roulette—and yes, of course, slots players—basically gamblers of all stripes, consistently losing because they don't come into the casinos with a winning attitude.

Does a good attitude affect the odds of the games or the machines? No. Whether you're the happiest leprechaun on earth or the sorriest loser this side of Suckersville, the odds are the odds. The slot machines won't care how you feel because they won't know. If you and I sit down to push the buttons ten times apiece, it won't matter which one of us pushes the button and sets the reels in motion. The result will be the same, regardless of your mood or your horoscope reading.

However, how you feel definitely does affect your overall chances of winning. A player that goes into the casino with the goal of winning does everything he or she can do to achieve that goal. This gambler will closely follow the money management advice we lay down in this section. They'll play within their means, they'll set reasonable limits, they'll control themselves at the machines, and when they're winning big, the casinos will see them at the cashier's cage converting their winnings into cash.

The losers, on the other hand, have defeat written all over them—in their actions, their moods, and of course, their results. No crowbar will pry these players away from the machines or tables until they've managed to lose their money. We've all seen plenty of these players.

To be sure, the casinos hold the edge at the slots and, in many places, a substantial edge. But players can still win, that is, the prudent players can.

Follow the advice in this section, and you'll be prudent too, the one gambler the casinos don't always feast on. You'll sometimes feast on them instead.

The next stop in money management is figuring out the correct bankroll for you, and playing within those limits.

2. BANKROLLING:
PLAY WITHIN YOUR MEANS

Determining the correct bankroll for you is not just about the money you can afford to risk at the tables from a financial point of view; it's also about what you can afford to lose emotionally. There is no rule more important in all of gambling. The possibilities of taking a loss are real, and if that loss will hurt, you're playing like a fool. It is inevitable that players who gamble over their heads will lose more than they can afford.

Luck won't help these players because even when the good music comes their way, as it surely will, they won't quit while they're ahead. They keep on going and going and going until the inevitable occurs.

By definition, the player that loses when he bets too much is getting into trouble. Don't let that player be you. Gambling with needed funds is a foolish gamble. However, if you never play over your head, you'll never suffer. Luck fluctuates in gambling. Sometimes you win, sometimes you lose. However, the goal for intelligent gamblers is to protect themselves in the times they lose and that means to set loss limits, not only for a particular session, but for an entire trip as well.

Let's go over some basic bankrolling principles.

a. Session Bankroll

The amount of money that you bring to the machines should be able to afford you two things:

1. The ability to handle a moderate size losing streak.

2. A decent amount of playing time to allow your luck to turn itself around and maybe swing your fortune in the other direction. That amount, which we'll discuss in a bit, will be your one-session bankroll.

The rule is this: If your session stake gets drained, you call it a day.

The key concept in formulating single-session bankrolls for a machine is to restrict losses to affordable amounts. That's why, when I discuss bringing money to a machine, I say to bring "moderate" amounts, not substantial amounts. Minimizing losses is the key. You can't always win. That's a fact of life for gamblers. Actually, that's a fact of life for everyone. If you're losing, keep the losses affordable—take a break. Don't let yourself get caught in a situation where you get beat badly. There's always another day.

You should have enough money at the machines to cover 200 plays. A play is the amount of money you'll be betting on one spin. For example, if you're playing 25¢ machines and are playing three credits at a time, your play costs 75¢ per spin. If you're playing a penny machine and covering 75 lines, your cost is also 75¢. Thus, your bankroll in both cases should be $150 for a session. If your credits instead added up to $1, then you would need a $200 machine stake (200 plays x $1). These are the maximum numbers. You can risk less, which you might want to do anyway, but you shouldn't risk more.

These conservative numbers are designed to keep your losses to affordable amounts. This doesn't mean that you'll lose the amounts shown above, only that you won't lose more than that. That's a big step in the right direction right there.

b. Trip Bankroll

A trip to a casino is really a multitude of individual sessions. For short trips, like a weekend jaunt, you may want to have enough to cover three to five sessions; for longer trips, say up to a week or two, five to seven sessions. The whole purpose of the trip bankroll is to have enough money to keep you playing through a particularly bad run of luck, and at the same time, to restrict your overall losses to "acceptable" amounts.

That's why I take such a conservative approach. By avoiding overbetting, you give yourself the opportunity to bounce back after bad luck. You also avoid wiping out your one-session stake or, even worse, digging deeper and deeper into your funds and running the risk of being totally destroyed.

Thus, using the figures worked out above, with an average play of 75¢, players should bring $450-$750 for a trip bankroll, depending upon the number of sessions they plan to play and $1 players should bring $600-$1,000. Players wagering more, or less, would adjust their numbers accordingly.

These bankroll amounts allow you to withstand any normal losing streak and still have the resources to play more and bounce back on top. If the numbers scare you, then you need to think about lower denomination machines. Money can be lost quickly at the machines—you probably know this already. It's better to play it safe than to be sorry.

3. PROTECT YOUR WINNING STREAKS

Protecting a winning streak is incredibly important if you want to be a winning player. Once you've accumulated a sizable win at the slot machines and have had a good run, the most important thing is to walk away a winner. There is no worse feeling than skulking away from a machine after having lost back all of your wins.

I recommend putting away three-fourths or more of your winnings into a "protected" area that you won't touch under any circumstances. That money is bankable, for you won't play it. Whether those wins are put aside into a "no touch zone," a mental note to shut off after you drop to a certain number of credits, or however you do it, make sure it gets done. Never touch the money you've set aside in your protected zone. Never. Protecting your wins is just as important as limiting your losses. Once the credits are on your side, it's your money, not the casinos. You risked and you won. Great. Now take it home with you and do something fun with it.

For example, let's say you're up $200 after a pretty good session at the penny slots. Put $150 of that money into your protected zone. Play out the remaining $50. This doesn't mean you have to lose the $50 if things turn sour; you can call it quits after $25 has been lost off of that, guaranteeing yourself an extra $25 win! But, in any case, don't dip below the $50 play zone. If that extra buffer is gone, you're gone, but with $150 to show for it!

If the $50 turns into more, keep going, keep accumulating, keep playing with the rest of your winnings, putting more aside as the wins accumulate. By doing this, your guaranteed winning pile steadily increases. Ride the cycle upwards. If the $200 mushrooms to $350, now move your protected zone to

$300 in winnings and play with the extra $50. If your bankroll still increases with more wins, put more aside again.

Once the winning streak stops and the tides of fortune turn against you, it's time to leave the machine—a guaranteed winner who can look back on that profitable session with great satisfaction.

Set no limits on a winning streak. When you've got a hot hand, ride it for all its worth. And when things cool down, chill yourself out with a cool drink over by the lounge.

4. EMOTIONAL CONTROL

Smart gamblers have one thing in common—they know how to manage their money and keep calm in the thick of the action, whether they're up and riding high, or struggling against a cold machine with the worst of luck. Superior playing skills alone does not make one a winning player. You must have self control. You must be able to keep the game in check and never lose sight of your goals, limits, and winning strategies.

Winning and losing streaks are a very real part of playing slots. It is how you deal with the inherent ups and downs at the machines that determine just how well you will fare at your sessions. You're going to lose sometimes. You're also going to win sometimes too. It is the smart gambler, the one who keeps it all under control, that will win big when he's winning and minimize losses when he's losing.

It's all about emotional control. You can't change the spins on the reel. You can, however, change your reactions to them.

REMEMBER: YOU'RE PLAYING FOR FUN

Gambling is a form of entertainment. If you cannot afford the possibility of losing, don't gamble at the stakes you were considering. Either play at lower levels or don't gamble at all. If playing the game causes you undue anxiety, for whatever the reason, then it ceases to be a form of entertainment and you need a break. Take some time away from the game, be it a coffee break or a month's rest.

Playing under anxiety not only ruins the fun of the game but can influence you to make decisions contrary to your best interests.

Your goal in gambling is not just to win but to get satisfaction out of playing the game. Keep that in mind and you can never go wrong.

You can't always win—even when the odds favor you—and you won't always lose, even when the odds are against you. In the short run, anything can happen and usually does. But over the long run, luck evens itself out. It is skill in the decisions you make and how you play the game that will determine your final results.

I'll show a simple example of how a loss of emotional control can quickly change a big winning session into a disaster. Let's say a player starts out with a bankroll of $200 and has been playing 25¢ machines. After two hours of tough play, he has ridden a surge of luck to $225 in winnings. Now he has $425 in front of him. Getting greedy and caught up in the excitement of the game, the gambler now really wants to put the squeeze on, so he goes against his pre-planned strategy, if he has one, and now goes for the $1 machines. With a little luck and a few big wins in a row, he'll be killing it—so he hopes.

After a bunch of losses, he gets frantic and goes for two machines at a time, pushing all his money out there. And now, more bad luck. Suddenly, a careful strategy that netted $225 got transformed into "if I can get lucky on this play, please" strategy. No surprise, the player loses all of his original stake and a bunch more. It's madness.

That's one story. Thankfully, there are more inspiring tales that we can profitably learn from.

While wandering around a particularly lively bank of slots, I ran into a couple, Bob and Maryanne, and got to shooting the breeze with them. They had been coming to Las Vegas for three decades and had been regular slots players over the years. As it turns out, they had once been blackjack players as well and had bought my book more than fifteen years previously. While they had some success at the twenty-one tables, the game couldn't hold their fancy. At heart, then and now they explained, they were dedicated slots players. They had played nothing else for the prior ten years. They loved the relaxation of the game—the fact that they could play the machines at their own pace with no dealer to hurry them along.

While Maryanne was mostly holding her own that day, Bob was really on a roll, and had already won $600 at the $1 slots. He was hoping to get up to $750, and then $1,000. The machine had been kind, and with a cold beer in his hand and two comp tickets to the dinner buffet stuffed into his back pocket, life was good. Bob's luck went up and down, and his bankroll slipped about a hundred as we spoke.

This was to be their last day before they flew back to their home in New Iberia, Louisiana (home of the Tabasco company), and they were hoping to ride out of town feeling extra good.

As I was watching, Bob almost caught the big one. The first two reels lined up like a dream, and the third, barely missing, made the spin a loser. Had it lined up for Bob, he would have won the big jackpot. He got a kick out of that and said to me, "I've seen more of them than you can shake a stick at. Well, that's it pod'ner. $500 is a good day. See you around." With that, Bob and Maryanne cashed out, and arm and arm took off for the cashier's cage and, presumably, the beginning of a good evening.

It was what I love to see: people playing to win and playing to have fun. Bob and Maryanne knew when to get up and walk away with their winnings.

5. STICK TO YOUR ORIGINAL LIMITS

The subject of sticking to your original limits is really a continuation of the discussion on bankrolling but important enough to merit its own section. Before sitting at machine and making your bets, you must not only decide on the amount of money you'll stake as a whole for the session but the max amount you will play per spin. This is important because escalating wagers can lead to escalating losses beyond what you are comfortable or even prepared to suffer.

You must restrict your losses to that predetermined amount. If you refuse to go against this rule you can never take a serious beating. It's as simple as that.

Never risk needed money at the machines, no matter how lucky you feel. Just as many "lucky" players contributed to the phenomenal growth of casinos as unlucky players. Well, perhaps there were, in fact, far more of the latter, but you get the point. The reality of gambling is that money can be lost, and if that money is earmarked for rent or food or any other necessity in your life, you're making a whopping mistake. I know this is all common sense, but it bears repeating because so many players go against this basic rule. There's an old Las Vegas saying about a guy who rides into town in a $20,000 Cadillac and leaves in a $100,000 Greyhound bus. Unfortunately, that saying bears a lot of truth. The list of sad stories from out-of-control gamblers is virtually unending with more stories getting added every day, lots more.

Let's say you're a quarter player and are on a winning streak that has expanded your starting machine bankroll for the day from $100 to $350, a nice $250 win. Should you go up to the $1 machine to really go for the kill? Absolutely not. You're hot and you're winning. The action is good. But raising your stake to the $1 machines now magnifies all the bets. Sure you can win a lot more. But you can also lose it all in no time at all. Don't let greed lead you astray. Greed nabs many gamblers and the end result is an unhappy player who got buried by that greed.

Bumping up in stakes over what you are comfortable with is dangerous. You can quickly wipe out all of your winnings at a level of play uncomfortable to you. A winning momentum can shift to a losing one and escalate rapidly when greed overcomes sanity. In such situations players can dig themselves into an inescapable hole. Betting over your head spells danger.

So many gamblers follow a reckless pattern that I honestly wonder what their goals really are. Are they really trying to win, or are they raising the stakes for nothing more than the adrenaline rush? They'll win, say $300, bump up the money (it could be at the slots, the table games or any other gamble), and if they don't get wiped out at the higher level, they may win again and bump up the stakes one more time. Well, it catches up quickly. Eventually, luck will turn. It always does. If these players were smart, they would get out while the getting was good. But inevitably, and almost invariably, they will not leave until they take the big fall.

What are these players really trying to do? The psychology on all of this is complex, but the empirical evidence is always the same. They lose it all back and then lose more again. There is almost no way that these gamblers can come out ahead because no matter how lucky they get, they raise the stakes so that all it takes is a small losing streak to wipe it all out—their winnings, their original stake, and then in desperation, even more.

I've seen it time and time again. And then these players say out loud to themselves: "What happened?"

Greed happened. Loss of control. You can do away with this recklessness. Stick to the level you started at so that luck changes, you stay a winner. It's okay to reach for the stars, but don't be jumping off the bridge to catch them. Whether you win or lose at slots, always keep to the level of betting you originally decided to play at.

HOW TO PROTECT YOURSELF AGAINST IMPULSE!

Some people have problems with self-control. They lose their planned stakes, and start digging for more money, which is trouble for them. Some people, actually many people, really get in trouble and lose all their available money. Here's my inside tips for protecting yourself:

1. Bring only the amount of money you're willing to lose and not a dollar more.

2. *Leave your ATM card at home, or if visiting, in your hotel room.*

This removes all possibilities of extra money coming into play and protects you from giving into impulse and making foolish decisions with your money.

HITTING A JACKPOT!

Every slots player's dream is to hit the monster jackpot. In fact, as more and more machines are linked together by big companies such as IGT, these jackpots get bigger and bigger, and more and more players get quite interested in taking a crack at it.

Well, what if you get lucky? Here's what you can expect. First of all, the casino will probably want to verify that the jackpot was struck legitimately. With all the angle players out there, the casino runs a constant battle to make sure that big wins are on the up and up. You'll need to fill out some forms for the IRS and show ID for verification. If your heart is racing wildly from the win, you'll have to do your best to calm down to get the formalities over with.

Most big jackpots will be paid out over twenty years in equal payments. Other jackpots may be paid in one lump sum, or a combination of large partial sums. How you will get paid depends upon the sponsoring company of the jackpot. (Usually it is not the casino running the progressive, but a large slots manufacturer such as IGT or Bally's). It's really not something you need to worry about until it happens.

You also have a choice of whether you want to remain anonymous or allow the casino to use the event to get publicity. If you want to be in the spotlight for a little bit, you can have some fun with this. The downside though, be forewarned, is that you might get bombarded by investment advisors and salesmen of every ilk, including con artists, all of whom are trying to help you spend your money. Long-lost friends, and ones not so long lost, might emerge out of the closet hoping you'll loan them some of the loot since you're so rich now.

In any case, if you do win the big one, you can start attending to your dreams. Life is about to get better.

HISTORY OF THE SLOT MACHINE

INTRODUCTION

The development of the slots industry and its first machine dates back about 100 colorful years, and got its start on the West Coast of the United States. Everything gets its start somewhere, and in the case of slots, it all began with one man.

Charles August Fey, a German immigrant who settled in San Francisco in the late nineteenth century, is credited with the invention of the slot machine as we know it today, with spinning reels and cash payoffs. Inspired by Gustav Schultze's poker gaming devices of the 1890s, which were found mainly in saloons and paid only cigars and free drinks, Fey devised a mechanical device in 1899 built of cast iron and called it the Liberty Bell.

Fey's original machine set the precedent for the entire line of future slots, with three reels containing symbols such as liberty bells, horseshoes and stars. The term "Bell" soon became the universal reference to all three-reel slot machines. The highest payoff was a set of three liberty bells. Following is the payout chart for his original machine.

1899 FEY LIBERTY BELL PAYOUT CHART

Symbols	# of Trade Checks
Three bells	20
Flush of hearts	16
Flush of diamonds	12
Flush of spades	8
Two horseshoes/One star	4
Two horseshoes	2

Other machines at the time used playing card suits and had three reels, each containing ten symbols. In 1901, Fey's first Draw Poker machine offered two plays for each nickel deposited, with an opportunity to win cigars for different card combinations. For example, players could win fifty cigars for a royal flush, ten cigars for four aces, and two cigars for three queens.

With pressure from players who wanted cash rewards, Fey eventually converted his machines to cash-paying games, making them the first three-reel slot machines to offer coin payouts.

Referred to as "drop card machines," a large number of earlier poker machines possessed only fifty playing cards, usually omitting the ten of spades and the jack of hearts. Without these two cards, the chance of getting a royal flush was reduced dramatically. The games accepted nickels for play, and the cards were attached to spinning drums that would flip them when the handle was pulled.

FEY'S POKER SLOT MACHINE PAYOUT CHART

Combination	Free Cigars
Royal Flush	50
Straight Flush	20
Four aces	10
Four kings	8
Four queens	7
Four under queens	5
Full hand	4
Flush	3
Straight	3
Three aces	3
Three kings	3
Three queens	2
Three under queens	2
Two pair aces up	2
Under aces	1
Two aces	1

THE BEGINNING OF MASS PRODUCTION

Fey made deals with saloon owners to place slots in their businesses, with an agreement to split the profits 50/50. At this time, machines sat directly on bar tops and returned 86% of coins, with a 14% profit that was divided between Fey and the saloon owner. Originally, Fey worked from his basement, building the games by hand and servicing the machines by horse and buggy, until he could no longer keep up with the construction of the machines alone.

In 1896, Fey opened a factory at 406 Market Street in San Francisco to meet the increasing demands from business owners.

Of course, with any popular invention comes a rush of anxious businessmen looking for a way to get their piece of the pie. One such businessman was Herbert Stephen Mills, an entrepreneur and successful manufacturer of various carnival games. Inspired by Fey's machines, Mills began mass-producing his own line of slots, patterning them after the original Liberty Bell.

In 1906, The Mills Novelty Company of Chicago was established, producing the Mills Liberty Bell, High Top, and Golden Falls. These games became popular immediately and were soon sold across the country to saloons, bowling alleys, pool parlors, and other businesses.

Around the same time, other manufacturers began producing large, freestanding, ornate wheel machines, which became the most popular cash slots for a period of time. The actual wheel resembled the wheel found on the modern-day television show Wheel of Fortune, with the exception that denominations were printed on the various colors. Fifty to one hundred colorful strips were found on the larger models. Players would select which color they wanted to play by depositing their coin into the desired slot. They would then pull a lever on the left side of the machine and wait anxiously to see if the arrow would land on their chosen color.

The Mills Company produced the first popular floor machine, called the Kalamazoo. This game gave players the option to insert one to five coins at a time and paid up to $1. When wheel machines proved to be successful, other manufacturers immediately began to produce their own versions of the original model while adding minor improvements. For example, Caille-Schiemer Co. produced the first six-coin game called The Puck, while the Mills Co. remained in the running with the first ten-coin game, The Duplex.

The Klondike, manufactured by Fey, was a smaller version of the wheel machines and sat directly on bar tops. The wheel exhibited six different colors: red, white, black, blue, yellow and green. A glass window at the front of the machine displayed the chosen color. Players could deposit up to six coins for their chance to win up to twenty-five drinks. The yellow strip paid twelve drinks, blue paid six, white three, green two, and red and black only one.

FEY'S KLONDIKE PAYOUT CHART

Color	Free Drinks
Yellow	12
Blue	6
White	3
Green	2
Red	1
Black	1

THE ROARING '20S

By 1927, the Mills Novelty Company became one of the nation's largest factories, employing over 1,000 people. There are many reasons for Mill's rapid success. He not only boosted sales through lowering prices, mail-order catalogues, and increased advertising, but also by making the games more aesthetically pleasing to players. The Mills machines had a glass window in the front of the game so that the player could actually see the monetary award waiting to gush out to the lucky winner.

Players were able to see three rows of symbols, which let them see just how close they had actually come to winning. Within forty years, over 500,000 Mills slot machines had been sold.

The prosperity during the Roaring Twenties led nickel machines to evolve into dime, quarter and half dollar machines. Because people were willing to play with larger denominations of money, manufacturers raced to produce and convert games that would accept larger sums. Caille Brothers developed the Superior Jackpot Bell in 1928, while Fey invented the Silver Dollar, the first Bell machine to allow players a chance to deposit a coin of that size.

1929 SILVER DOLLAR PAYOUT CHART
5¢ MACHINE

Combination	Payout
Three Bars	20
Three Bells	16
Two Bells/One Bar	16
Three Plums	12
Two Plums/One Bar	12
Three Oranges	8
Two Oranges/One Bar	8
Two Cherries/One Lemon	4
Two Cherries/One Bell	4
Two Cherries	2

The 1920s also marked the beginning of jackpot displays that allowed players to see large amounts of money waiting to be won. The coins were visible through one or two windows positioned in the front of the machine. During this time, cast iron machines were converted to aluminum machines.

Within thirty years of Fey's invention of slots machines in 1899, over a million slot machines had been manufactured worldwide.

THE '30S, '40S, AND '50S

1931 through 1941 marked the Golden Age of Slots. Prohibition gave rise to the notorious speakeasies—illegal hangouts that served alcohol and housed slot machines. The sale of slots soared during this period, with an annual revenue of approximately $150 million. Although politicians and law enforcement agencies fought against these gaming devices, slots continued to increase in popularity. During the Depression, hopeful players flocked to the machines for a chance to hit the jackpot.

In 1935, Watling Manufacturing introduced the ROL-A-TOR, a slot machine that showed the last nine coins deposited through a large rotary devise at the top of the game. The name changed to ROL-A-TOP the following year, and in no time almost every manufacturer had its own version of this type of game.

During the 1940s, World War II was raging, which affected the manufacturing of slots. Many slot machine facilities converted to war production manufacturing plants. Shortages of aluminum caused slot machine manufacturers to return to cast iron designs. In 1942, the manufacturing of slot machines stopped completely until the war ended.

The end of the 1940s and the beginning of the 1950s produced a unique type of attention-getting slot machines. Frank Polk, a reputable artist, created a line of carved wooden statues to encase slot machines such as the Mills High-Tops. The figures were intricate, life-like designs in the form of cowboys, Indians, miners and other western figures. Like many of the other earlier machines, these unique slot machines are collector's items and have a whole legion of enthusiasts collecting, trading, buying and selling these vintage goodies.

THE '60S & '70S:
THE ELECTROMECHANICAL ERA

In the 1960s, Bally's Manufacturing, which had concentrated on arcade machines and other coin-operated devises since the 1930s, began to successfully design and produce slot machines. Their machines were unique in that they utilized electromechanical circuitry to recognize a large number of payout possibilities. They also replaced the single-coin "slicer" of earlier machines with a hopper payout devise.

Bally's 1963 Money Honey machine possessed an ingenious hopper unit that was able to contain 2,500 dimes. Left-to-right and right-to-left payouts, as well as five-line machines, are credited to these innovations. Bally's accomplishments of the 1960s pushed them to the forefront of manufacturing throughout the next decade. Bally's controlled 90% of the slot machine market in Nevada during the 1970s and also profited by overseas sales.

In 1967, a significant development in design came with the production of Bally's famous "809," the first slot machine to give players an option to play more than one coin at a time while getting proportional winning payouts for the additional coins. The 809 allowed up to five-coin play. Each additional coin deposited in the machine increased the payout amount.

Casinos that had originally scoffed at this new idea soon saw it for what it was—a moneymaker that greatly increased a player's excitement and the casino's bottom line.

BALLY'S 1967 809 SLOT MACHINE

Symbol	1st Coin	2nd Coin	3rd Coin	4th Coin	5th Coin
3 Bars	$10	$20	$30	$40	$50
3 Melons	$7.50	$15	$22.50	$30	$37.50
3 Stars	$5	$10	$15	$20	$25

THE '80S & '90S: THE COMPUTER AGE

In the 1980s, Bally's manufactured a series of machines called the "Series E." These omitted the electromechanical circuitry and replaced it with the technologically superior microprocessor. These devices were more reliable than their predecessors and were easier to maintain. Around this same time, music chips were inserted in the microprocessor, adding to the appeal of the game. People were not only enticed by the attractive designs on the machines, but were also engaged by the new sounds that occurred when coins were inserted and the reels were spun.

Microprocessors, or "chips," controlled the entire workings of the machine, from the coin meters to the intricate symbols. Stored in the memory, chips contain information on how often the machine was played, the last time it paid out, and the amount that it paid out. Microprocessors are the brains of today's slot machines.

BALLY'S 1983 E2088—S1 SLOT MACHINE

1st Coin
Cherry/Cherry = $5
Cherry = $1

2nd Coin
Bell/Bell/Bell or Bar = $20
Orange/Orange/Orange or Bar = $10

3rd Coin
3 Bars = $100

4th Coin
3 $1,000 Symbols = $1,000

While Bally's is still a major player in the slots market, It Is no longer the player. That title belongs to IGT, International Game Technology. This Reno-based manufacturer dominates the industry with a massive worldwide presence and many of the most popular slot machines. Older popular machines like the Double Diamond and Triple Diamond machines, the Red, White and Blue series, and its Sizzling Sevens and Wild Cherries machines dominated casino floors.

When IGT introduced its Wheel of Fortune design, it became a huge hit. This fun machine has payouts for various winning combinations, but the real excitement comes when you line up the three Wheel of Fortune symbols. Then the Wheel of Fortune displayed above the machine spins, with the possibilities of you winning anywhere from twenty-five all the way up to 1,000 times on its progressive.

But as it had for the hundred plus years since Fey's original slot machine, progress and evolution would revolutionize the landscape. And then came the penny slots…

THE 2000S: PENNY SLOT DOMINATION

The widely popular penny video slots started to take hold of the gaming market in the 1990s and completely dominated the market by the early 2000s. These video slots, with all the gimmickry made possible by the advance in computer technology, created a lot of fun for players while the allure of playing cheaply, at just a penny a pitch, made a perfect partnership.

As we have learned penny slots are not a penny a pitch and are in fact expensive machines to play for the most part, but just the same, they are the most popular machines in play today. The combination of the huge selection of paylines—each one representing a potential winner—and the vast array of colorful themed machines gives players lots of ways to be entertained.

THE EVOLUTION OF SLOTS AND THE FUTURE

Slot machines have come a long way from Fey's Liberty Bell. While some of the original concepts have remained, such as the reels and some of the symbols, time has marched forward. From nickel-ante type machines paying out cigars, cigarettes, drinks and modest winnings, the stakes and prizes have now become enormous. Chances to win millions of dollars and other expensive prizes and are now the lures. The slot machine craze that began with Charles Fey building machines in his basement has exploded into a billion-dollar industry.

Manufacturers have added flashing lights, entertaining video sequences, and various attention-getting features to compete for the coins of hopeful players. Devices have been added for convenience: credit card and bill acceptors, buttons for rapid and easy play, and options to utilize accrued winnings instead of having to continuously insert money. Machines accept multiple credits for play, and progressives linked with banks of machines, not only within a casino but among a group of casinos, have added a new dimension. There are also machines with multiple payout lines and wild symbols.

The fundamentals of determining winning combinations have also completely evolved. Keeping in tune with the computer age, slot machines are microprocessor based, running on chips and sophisticated programs that track everything from time played and average bet to number of combinations won and average yield over any number of variables. Payouts are no longer in cash but get credited on a paper ticket that can be redeemed at the cashier or played in other machines. That's a long way from the strictly mechanical machines of the early days. But as they say, the more things change the more they stay the same. The slots are still the slots. And players still like them and play them.

Whatever changes may come over the next 100 years, in all likelihood gamblers will still be playing the slots, which may be activated by buttons, visual cues, or even brain waves. I can't see far enough ahead to know the methods, but I can see far enough behind to know they'll still be around and players will still be playing them and trying to beat them.

LEGAL MILESTONES FOR SLOTS

Although a billion-dollar industry today, slot machines have had to endure many setbacks and bombardments throughout the years. On April 18, 1906, a tremendous earthquake rocked San Francisco and the surrounding area. The entire San Francisco slots manufacturing base was devastated. In no time, however, the industry bounced right back into business.

Various religious groups interpreted the natural disaster as a sign from God concerning the sinfulness and evils of the slots-playing world. These groups fought to outlaw not only slot machines, but also liquor and saloons. With pressure from many different directions, slot machines were outlawed in San Francisco in 1909. Nevada followed in 1910, and the entire state of California in 1911. Soon many other states followed.

Manufacturers refused to become deterred by these new laws, so they decided to relocate to the East Coast. In 1912, Nevada legalized slots only as trade stimulators, with the stipulation that the machines could not pay out any monetary awards. Machines such as the Caille Gum Vendor, made by the Caille Brothers, were produced to offer prizes like candy or gum. These machines enticed women and children to play, which was socially frowned upon, creating an immediate uproar. If a woman was seen chewing gum, people automatically assumed that she had been playing the slot machines, which led to the social taboo of gum-chewing for women.

One of the more popular trade stimulators was the Liberty Bell Gum Fruit Model, produced in 1910. This was simply a typical slot machine with a gum vendor attached on the side to dispense winnings. The symbols represented the various flavors of the gum: spearmint, lemon, orange and plum. Many slot machines today continue to utilize the fruit symbols, and the original stick of gum symbol has evolved into the "bar" as we know it today. The lemon found on these machines actually gave rise to referring to malfunctioning cars as "lemons."

The battle against saloons and slot machines were led by groups such as the Anti-Saloon League and the Women's Christian Temperance Union. These groups pressured the government, finally becoming victorious on August 1, 1917 when the Senate passed a resolution to create the 18th Amendment, which outlawed the manufacturing, distribution, sale and use of alcohol. On January 16, 1920, this resolution became law.

With Prohibition came an enormous boom in the slots business, with an ebbing in the popularity of the gum-vending machines. During Prohibition, the majority of the speakeasies relied on slot machines for up to 20% of their profits.

A break for slot manufacturers came in 1931 when Nevada legalized gambling. Drinking was then legalized in 1933, but slots remained illegal in the other states. In 1934, New York's Mayor LaGuardia made an impact on the gambling world by hurling over 1,000 machines into the ocean. Orders were given to destroy all slot machines on the spot, no matter what. Slots manufacturers, however, remained in business full throttle by building gambling ships in offshore waters equipped with slot machines and table games. The "Golden Age of Slots" ended during World War II due to the conversion of slots manufacturing factories into war production facilities. When the war ended, the demand for slot machines immediately rose again.

During the 1950s, the Strip in Las Vegas and the city of Reno began to thrive. In 1951, however, Congress passed the Johnson Act, which terminated all interstate slot-machine shipping to enforce the laws against slots. While shipping continued to states that allowed such interstate commerce, it had a negative effect on business in the non-legal states.

To various degrees, this ban continues even into the 2000s, more than fifty years later. Most states allow the collection of slot machines for personal use (about eight don't allow slot machines of any type for any reason), but only according to varying legal definitions. Generally speaking, you're allowed to own slot machines if they are "antiques," which, again depending on the state, could be anything from ten to thirty years old, to machines manufactured only before 1941, as in South Dakota.

You'll need to check on applicable laws before venturing into these waters.

In 1976, the slots manufacturers got a big boon when the state of New Jersey decided to allow machines in Atlantic City. Further boons came in the '80s and '90s as the Mississippi riverboat states followed suit, Indian reservations opened casinos nationwide, and manufacturers began heavily courting business in overseas markets.

While slot machines are not legal for gambling use in states everywhere, business is certainly booming, and the industry is healthy and growing. Imagine this: More than $100 billion dollars is wagered on slots every year in the United States alone. Yes, this is a big industry.

BE A WINNER

The key to beating the slots, as in all gambling pursuits, is to play only the games that give you the best chances of winning. Your chances of coming out ahead at the slots are in direct proportion to the payout percentage. The greater the payout percentage set on the machine you're playing, the better chance you have of walking away with a profit; the worse the odds (payout percentage) of the machine, the harder it will be for you to win.

For example, a machine that pays back 99% gives you a very good chance of riding just a little luck into profits. On the other hand, a machine that pays only 50% will take your money so fast that you'll need a lot more than luck to get ahead. A house edge of 50% is just too steep, even 90% is too hard to crack. But that's not the norm you'll face. In slots-friendly casinos, you'll often be playing in the mid to upper 90% range at the quarter or better machines, giving you a far better chance of winning than just about all slots players.

We've gone over all the winning techniques and secrets in this chapter, how to find the best paying machines, how to manage your money, and many other important concepts.

It's now up to you to play smart and be a winner!

GLOSSARY

Action—The total amount of money played measured by the sum of all bets placed. Thus, betting a quarter 100 times, would be equivalent to $25.00 in action, or betting $1 for 700 plays adds up to $700 in action.

Average Payer—A machine that is neither tight, nor loose, but in between.

Bank, Bank of Machines—This is a group of machines connected together in a structure as a design unit.

Bar—A popular symbol on slot machines. This symbol is often found as one bar, two bars, and three bars.

Big Bertha—The gigantic slot machines of many reels, usually eight to ten, that are strategically placed by casinos near their front entrance (usually, but not always) to lure curious players into their casinos for a pull or two.

Big Coin Machine—A slot machine requiring $5, $25, or larger credits to play.

Big Coin Player—A slots player who plays $5, $25, or larger credits.

Blanks—The stops on a reel that contain no symbols, thus, blank stops, or blanks.

Bonus Round—A free spin which is activated by hitting combinations that trigger the bonus round.

Buy-Your-Pay—A machine with a single payout line that will only pay on certain symbols if enough credits are played.

Cage—The cashier's cage, where players can exchange chips for cash, change traveler's checks, or convert cashout vouchers to cash.

Change Booth—Formerly, a booth set up for the specific purpose of changing players' bills into credits, or their credits into bills. The change booth has gone extinct.

Changeperson—The casino employee who services the machines area for the purpose of changing bills into credits. Also called **slots attendant**.

Carousels—An oval or round-shaped area containing a bank of machines. A changeperson often sits enclosed in the center space..

Cashout Button—This button, when pressed, releases all the credits that were won, or at least held by the machine.

Club Booths—An area in the casino specifically set up to sign and service members of a player's club.

Cold—A machine that is paying out less than expected, or a player who is on a losing streak.

Comp—Short for complimentary. The freebies given out by the casino, usually as a reward for play.

Denomination—The size of credit (or bill) used to play a particular machine. 1¢, 5¢, 25¢, and $1, are the most popular denominations found. Increasingly, larger denominations such as $5, $25, $100, and even higher are found now as well.

Extended Paytable—On slot machines, when the paytable showing winning combinations extends below the play buttons, on the "belly glass."

Five Line Criss Cross—A multiple payline machine that has five winning directions, three horizontal and two diagonal.

Hit Frequency—The expected frequency of winning payouts that a slot machine will produce. For example, if a winning combination will hit, on average, one time in six, the hit frequency will be 16.67%.

Hold—The percentage or actual dollar amounts a casino wins from its players. Also known as Hold Percentage.

Hot—A machine that is paying out better than expected, or a player who is on a winning streak.

House Edge—See House Percentage.

House Percentage—The mathematical amount a casino can expect to win over a large number of trials. Also known as house edge, vigorish or vig.

Jackpot—The big win on any machine—the jackpot!

Local Area Progressive (LAP)—Progressive slot machines linked together within a casino and typically owned and operated by that casino. Also called Proprietary Progressives.

Liberty Bell—The original slots machine invented by Charles Fey. Also, a symbol on the reels of many slot machines.

Long Run—The concept of what certain results are expected to be when occurring over many trials, thus, in the long run.

Loose Machine—A slot machine marked by frequent winners, or a high percentage payback to the players—as opposed to a tight machine.

Loose Payer—See Loose Machine.

Max Credit Button—The button, when pushed, that plays all credits allowed.

Medium Coin Machine—A 50¢ or $1 denomination machine.

Medium Coin Player—A player who plays the 50¢ or $1 denomination machines.

Mega-Progressive—A super-jackpot progressive that can get as high as millions of dollars. See Progressives.

Mills Machines—An early machine, manufactured by Mills, an early slot innovator and producer, that was the first to use the fruit symbols and have a jackpot.

Money Management—The strategy used by smart players to wisely manage their money while gambling so as to preserve their capitol, avoid big losses, and manage their wins.

Monster Jackpot—An enormous jackpot.

Multiple Payline—A slot machine with more than one winning payline.

Multiple Progressives—A machine that contains more than one progressive jackpot.

Multiplier—A multiple credit slot machine that pays proportionately more on winning combinations for each credit played.

One-Armed Bandit—A colorful slang term used for slot machines.

One Credit Button—The button that plays one credit when pushed. The spin reels button will need to be pushed afterwards to spin the reels.

Payback or Payout Percentage—The expected long-term return percentage for money wagered. A 97% payback states that the expected return on every dollar bet will be 97¢, for a loss of 3¢.

Payline—The line on the glass over the reels of the machine, behind which the symbols need to line up to be a winning combination.

Payout—A button on slot machines that, when pressed, issues coins or credits to the player if they have been accrued on the machine. Also, the amount that will be paid if a winning combination is hit.

Paytable—The display on the slot machine showing winning combinations and their payouts.

Payout Meter—The display on the machine that shows the number of credits played and won on a spin.

Penny Machine—A slot machine that can be played in increments of 1¢ per play—the most popular type slot machine today.

Progressive Machines, Progressives—Progressives feature a jackpot that increases each time a credit is inserted into any slots machine that is hooked up to the progressive meter. When the jackpot does hit, the lucky player wins the total accumulated in the jackpot, and the jackpot total will be reset to a predetermined starting point.

Proprietary Progressives—See **Local Area Progressives**.

Rating—An evaluation received by a player from the casino stating the level of action the player gives the casino.

Reels—The spinning mechanism containing the symbols on a slot machine. Technically, called Stepper Reels.

Short Run—A brief sequence of events, where anything can happen, even though the odds say they may not be likely.

Single Coin Machine—A slot machine that accepts only a single credit for play. Rarely, if ever, found today.

Single Payline Machine—A slot machine with only one payline that determines winners.

Slot Machines—A mechanical or microchip-driven gambling machine that accepts bets in the form of credits, spins reels, and disperses wins according to the combinations of symbols which match those as shown on a printed paytable.

Slots—Short for Slot Machines.

Slots Host—The person responsible for taking care of the slots players and their needs.

Slots Palace—A casino that only has slot machines as its gambling games.

Small Coin Machine—A 1¢, 5¢, 10¢, or 25¢ denomination machine.

Small Coin Player—A player who plays the 1¢, 5¢, 10¢, or 25¢ denomination machines.

Standalone progressive (SAP)—A type of progressive machine that is not linked to any other machine and the full value of the progressive jackpot grows as a result of credits played on its machine.

Start—On some machines, pushing this button will spin the reels if credits are already bet.

Stepper Reels—See Reels.

Symbols—The various markings on a slot machine reel, such as fruits, bells and bars.

Ticket-In/Ticket-Out—All modern video slot machines convert accrued credits into a ticket that can be redeemed for money, or inserted into another machine. These machines, and this process, are called TICKET-IN/TICKET-OUT.

Tight Machine—A slot machine marked by infrequent winners, or a low percentage payback to the players. This is opposed to a loose machine that has a high percentage payback.

Tight Payer—See Tight Machine.

TITO—See Ticket-In Ticket-Out Machines.

Tokes—Tipping, in casino parlance.

Vig—See House Percentage.

Vigorish—See House Percentage.

Wide Area Progressive—A progressive slot machine that is linked up with other such machines across the state and whose jackpot swells each time a credit is played in any of the machines linked together.

Wild Play Machines—A slot machine that uses wild symbols to multiply the winning payouts.

Wild Symbol—The symbol earmarked as "wild" could be designated as any winning symbol for the benefit of the player, or in addition, can increase the normal winning payout by a multiple.

Window—The glass area in the front of the machine where the player views the symbols and reels.

LEVEL III LOTTO WHEELS
50% OFF!!!

The advanced **Level III lotto wheel packages** are specifically designed to work with the advanced Level III strategies in the colored papers' series. They feature one-key, two-key and three-key wheels in a variety of combinations—from 7-18 chosen-number combinations and purchases of 5-25 tickets—and are built to give you optimum coverage of Level III chosen numbers and power keys extracted from the Level III strategies.

These **professional-level lotto wheels** are formulated for players looking to optimize their chosen numbers coverage with the goal of hitting huge, monster jackpots!

Level III Emerald Lotto 6-Ball Wheel Package
50 Powerful 6-Ball Wheels $50, Just $24.95!
The emerald package includes 50 professional 6-ball wheels covering a variety of your chosen number, ticket purchase, and key packages as described above.

Level III Diamond Lotto 6-Ball Wheel Package
100 Powerful 6-Ball Wheels $100, Just $49.95!
The diamond package includes 100 professional 6-ball wheels covering a variety of your chosen number, ticket purchase, and key packages as described above.

Level III Sapphire Lotto 5-Ball Wheel Package
50 Powerful 5-Ball Wheels $50, Just $24.95!
The sapphire package includes 50 professional 5-ball wheels covering a variety of your chosen number, ticket purchase, and key packages as described above.

Level III Ruby Lotto Wheel Package
100 Powerful 5-Ball Wheels $100, Just $49.95!
The ruby package includes 100 pro 5-ball wheels with a bank of chosen number, ticket, and key packages, plus a section with wheels for super aggressive players and syndicates (10-20 chosen numbers, 20-100 tickets) seeking jackpots worth $100s of millions.

Level III Treasure of Jewels
Emerald, Diamond, Sapphire, Ruby—$300, Just $150, now $124.95!!!
All the jewels together—Emerald, Diamond, Sapphire, Ruby—for **50% off** $300. Now just $150! Reduced $25 again! **$175 OFF** total for readers of this book!!! Only $124.95!